T0161873

Dear Sister

Endorsements

Where does saying yes to God lead us? For Cadey Fenn, it was to be a foster parent. Cadey's life-changing story goes beyond fostering and into the blessings God has waiting for each of us within an obedience journey. Every chapter not only unfolds her story, but the reader's as well.

--Bob Goff
Author of New York Times bestsellers
Love Does and *Everybody, Always*

"Cadey's vulnerability and authenticity in this beautiful book is a gift. Her inspiring story is deeply moving, and her passion for life is contagious. This book will open your heart and sharpen your faith as you discover and uncover your limitless potential to impact the kingdom of God in both the extraordinary and ordinary moments of life."

--Kayla Stoecklein
Author of *Fear Gone Wild*, Speaker, & Mental Health Advocate

Cadey gracefully articulates the beauty and brokenness of the adoption journey. This care chronicle forces us all to deal with our own humanity and brokenness. I'm thankful for writers like Cadey who can eloquently and gently invite you into their story in order to find your own.

--Jeff Gokee
Executive Director of Phoenix One

In *Dear Sister*, Cadey Fenn takes us on a vulnerable and real journey of one woman who said yes to God—a yes that not only forever changed her life but the life of a child. Though this book gives insight into the foster care system, it really is an invitation to draw us all more deeply into the story of how God has fostered us into his love and how God's love can save a life.

--Debbie Alsdorf
Author of *It's Momplicated*, *The Faith Dare*, and *Deeper*

Through Cadey's pen, you will embark on a journey of an ordinary family who was invited into a step of extraordinary faith. *Dear Sister* will invite each of us into identifying the beautiful opportunities to trust God to take action with the courageous invitations in our stories, too.

--Brian Wurzell
Worship Pastor &
Promise Tangeman-Wurzell
CEO and Creative Director of
the Web Design Company, GoLive

Wow, wow, wow. This book is finally here, and it is incredible. *Dear Sister* takes us on the beautiful yet difficult journey that comes with fostering and adoption. We read about brokenness, healing, restoration, love, and of course God's faithfulness through it all.

--Rich Baker
Pastor of Communities,
Arbor Road Church, Long Beach California

Dear Sister,

A JOURNEY OF TRANSFORMATION IN FOSTERING THE ORPHANED HEART

CADEY FENN

NASHVILLE

NEW YORK • LONDON • MELBOURNE • VANCOUVER

Dear Sister

A Journey of Transformation in Fostering the Orphaned Heart

© 2022 Cadey Fenn

All rights reserved. No portion of this book may be reproduced, stored in a retrieval system, or transmitted in any form or by any means—electronic, mechanical, photocopy, recording, scanning, or other—except for brief quotations in critical reviews or articles, without the prior written permission of the publisher.

Published in New York, New York, by Morgan James Publishing. Morgan James is a trademark of Morgan James, LLC. www.MorganJamesPublishing.com

Proudly distributed by Ingram Publisher Services.

All Scripture taken from THE HOLY BIBLE, NEW INTERNATIONAL VERSION®, NIV® Copyright © 1973, 1978, 1984, 2011 by **Biblica, Inc.**® Used by permission. All rights reserved worldwide.

Morgan James BOGO™

A **FREE** ebook edition is available for you or a friend with the purchase of this print book.

CLEARLY SIGN YOUR NAME ABOVE

Instructions to claim your free ebook edition:
1. Visit MorganJamesBOGO.com
2. Sign your name CLEARLY in the space above
3. Complete the form and submit a photo of this entire page
4. You or your friend can download the ebook to your preferred device

ISBN 9781631958021 paperback
ISBN 9781631958038 ebook
Library of Congress Control Number:
2021948404

Cover Design by:
Chris Treccani
www.3dogcreative.net

Interior Design by:
Christopher Kirk
www.GFSstudio.com

Morgan James is a proud partner of Habitat for Humanity Peninsula and Greater Williamsburg. Partners in building since 2006.

Get involved today! Visit MorganJamesPublishing.com/giving-back

Dedication

To the love of my life and partner in everything,
you are my greatest gift.
I love you with my whole heart, Cory Fenn.

Contents

Acknowledgments

I thank God for continually placing people in my life who not only held me up so I could keep going, but encouraged me to write it all down.

To my husband and kids, thank you for believing in me. Thank you for allowing me to lock myself in my office for hours at a time so I could write. Thank you for the moments you barged in to give me a hug or a love note. My deepest desire for each of you is for you to see you too are capable of hard but incredible things!

To my parents, it is because of you that Sister is who she is today. It takes a village, and you never wavered from stepping in to care, pray, and love my family.

To my family, I am beyond blessed to have each of you cheering me on, loving my family, and believing in us every step of the way.

Sammie, you mean the world to me and my family. None of this would have been possible without you loving and serving my family.

Kara, you have cheered me on through the hardest moments, the victories, and the long nights—reminding me this too is an act of obedience to God. Love you, friend.

Megan, you believed in me before I ever believed I could write this book. You read the words I had written in their rawest form and pushed me to keep going. You are such a gift. I am forever grateful for your honest, loving, and empowering words to me.

Rita Halter Thomas, you are not just an editor. You have coached me, prayed over me, and pushed me forward in times I wanted to give up. The time I have spent with you, grueling over these pages and learning from your expertise, has been beyond anything I could have imagined. Your partnership took my manuscript and made it into something beyond my dreams. Your talent and dedication to *Dear Sister* have gone above and beyond. I am forever grateful, and now I see why God put us together.

Morgan James Publishing team, your partnership and commitment to *Dear Sister,* and me, has been over and above my expectations. Your team saw potential in this book, and I am forever thankful. From your feedback to long conference calls contributing to every detail of this book, it has been such an honor to work with each of you.

Foreword

Risky obedience is one of the most commonly overlooked actions of living out our faith. When you take risks like obeying God, you have the potential to see God show up, because you need Him to. I wonder if the reason we don't see God's power at play in our lives is because we play it too safe. I'm with Matt Chandler on this one: "Comfort is the god of our generation."

Faith welcomes obedience and obedience requires risk. And we kind of hate the idea of risk. I mean, c'mon, it's risky. Yet, we're daily instructed to study God's Word, hearing His invitation to a life of faith. Yet, it's easier to be content studying it or watching sermons about other people's faith, failing to live a life of risky obedience ourselves that faith supposes.

In *Risk is Right*, Pastor John Piper writes, *"A choice lies before you: Either waste your life or live with risk. Either sit on the sidelines or get in the game. After all, life was no cakewalk for Jesus, and he didn't promise it would be any easier for his fol-*

lowers. We shouldn't be surprised by resistance and persecution. Yet most of us play it safe. We pursue comfort. We spend ourselves to get more stuff. And we prefer to be entertained. We are all tempted by the idea of security, the possibility of a cozy Christianity with no hell at the end. But what kind of life is that really? It's a far cry from adventurous and abundant, from truly rich and really full, and it's certainly not the heights and the depths Jesus calls us to." [1]

Dear Sister is an autobiographical story of risky obedience, a story God called us all to live. Noah overlooked taunts from others to obey and build an arc. Abraham left everything behind, placed his only son on a sacrificial altar, all for obedience. Gideon fought with the odds stacked against him, prophets called out judgement upon entire people groups, Peter stepped onto a storm, the disciples left their life's work, Paul risked his life (and lost it), and then there's Cadey. And then there's you. God is continually calling all of His followers (you and me both) to step out in obedient faith amidst living in a culture that commends safety, conformity and security.

Cadey's journey of welcoming a strong-willed, curly-haired uncertainty into her home is a story of risky, obedient faith. It is simultaneously an invitation for each of us to live beyond our capacity, because we can find God there. God hangs out at places beyond our power, places that require His. He is in the deep waters, so to speak. If all we ever do is splash around in the shallows, we'll never see the power of God at work. That, I'm convinced, is why so few people see God working in their lives. They genuinely don't think they need Him.

Dear Sister is a modern-day story of the church, a story that is still being written. We, dear readers, are collectively called to listen and boldly respond with extraordinary obedience to whatever God is calling us to. This life of faith in Jesus will require dependence. It will require patience. It will require apologies because of our tendencies toward selfishness. Yet, it's worth it. The Kingdom has come, will come, and can come in our homes as it is in heaven. The story of the modern-day church is our story. Let's join in on the adventure of risky, obedient faith. What do you have to lose? You'll find out in these pages, it's everything you've been hoping to lose all along.

Megan Fate Marshman
Author of *Meant For Good* and *SelfLess*
Author, Speaker and Pastor

Introduction

Welcome to the most honest and vulnerable words I have ever written. In the following pages, you will join me on an incredible journey of obedience to the Lord—from the weight of saying yes to freedom experienced.

I desire to honor those with a story of their own to tell—like my daughter—but share my journey of loss, pain, and uncertain identity tethered together with a rebirth of joy, mercy, and faith. As onlookers, we see the heroism in foster and adoptive parents, but as you join me, I will give you an intimate look at the ways God transforms hearts through obedience. I will remind you we can neither see all the things God is doing nor can we know all His plans.

Ever felt as if God wanted you to do something impossible? Maybe you thought, "Who me? Wrong!"

Maybe you thought this because the task in front of you stretches completely beyond your wheelhouse. Perhaps you made a mental list with the names of all the people more qualified. Perhaps fear bogged you down and doubt kept you awake at night. I know I am not the only one raising a hand right now. God loves to write unexpected stories, using the least qualified people to produce the most incredible things.

Why *Dear Sister*?

It all began with love letters to my foster daughter, Sister. We call her Sister because, if you could see her sweet little angel face and the cascade of bouncy curls swirling around in all her constant motion, I think you would find it's the perfect nickname. With every letter I wrote to her, the truths and blessings I poured over her began to seep deep within my soul. I soon discovered all the truths and blessings she needed were needs of my own.

I held those letters for myself as if they needed to be locked away in a diary with the key thrown away—each one so raw and intimate with details of my personal brokenness. I believed the lie for too long. I feared if anyone saw, they would believe what I believed about myself—I wasn't good enough, strong enough, or smart enough. So, when God asked me to share them with all of you, it took years for me to be brave, to face my insecurities and all the lies I've believed about myself, and to conquer them. After all, if I cannot reassure you that saying yes to God is worth all you will face in this world, and if I cannot convince you that you can overcome, I might as well lock the letters away to collect dust in the deepest corner of my closet. I can honestly say the bravery of embracing vulnerability set me free. Just knowing this story of love, obedience, grace, and loss doesn't need to stop here encourages me. Knowing my experience with the Lord may touch the hearts of others and encourage them into obedient action warms my soul.

Let me reassure you, you are not alone in feeling frozen from fear and vulnerability. As you journey with me through this book, it is my prayer you will brave the deep and scary waters of impossibilities with me.

Hope They Like My Shoes

I once spoke at a women's conference and as I prepared to leave the house, I chose a brand-new outfit that had been hanging in the closet for a special occasion. This seemed special enough, so I rushed to change. Once on, I looked down at my bare feet, unmanicured and needing something sparkly on them to finish the outfit. While super cute, the three-inch leather pumps I picked would practically eat my feet alive standing in them for hours. I meant to save them for a hot date with my husband, not a long day on my feet. The day was barely starting and already turning into a disaster. This was not me. I am not someone who loves heels and a pencil skirt, more often I prefer my lulu stretch pants and a cozy sweater.

As I left the house, my thoughts focused on how I looked and the impression I'd make—needing the ladies attending to notice my cuteness and approve. However, the whole "put-to-gether outfit of cuteness" served as a disguise and distraction from a damaging truth in my heart behind the whole matter. I didn't need my audience-of-the-day to approve of my outfit. I needed them to approve of *me*.

How often do we dress up not because we love ourselves or want to feel confident, but because we don't feel confident in ourselves at all? The shoes, the mask of makeup on my face, the pretty clothes, none of it was for me. It was all an attempt to gain the acceptance of the audience around me.

As I walked on stage, I looked down at my shoes and realized all the morning energy I spent stressing over how I looked left me overlooking who I was representing. I spent so much time and effort worrying about my reflection in the mirror I forgot who I needed to be reflecting. At that moment, I realized I needed to get out of the way and allow them to see more than me. They needed to see Jesus. I mean, wasn't that the whole point?

So, as I stood there in front of hundreds of women, I blurted, "Ladies, I am going to take my shoes off."

I placed the microphone onto the floor of the stage, bent down, and took those tight shoes off my feet. Standing barefoot, I placed the shoes at the front of the stage so everyone could see them. I reclaimed the microphone. An uncomfortable silence filled the air as I scanned the room. The ladies' faces reflected confusion and even a bit of disgust. I guess not everyone appreciates bare feet.

After another quiet moment, I spoke. I explained how I had been so worried about how I looked, and those silly shoes, I had not only forgotten Jesus, but I had also forgotten who I was. I hate fancy shoes. I needed to be the me God created *me* to be and allow these ladies to feel the freedom to pursue who God created *them* to be. Nothing illuminates more powerfully than seeing someone confident in their own unique identity—the identity given to them by Christ.

I watched in awe as something miraculous happened. One woman leaned down and started removing her shoes. Another followed, and yet another, until every woman in the room followed suit and placed their shoes in front of them. What a powerful statement, as if to say you are not alone, no more pretending, no more uncomfortable facades, no more acting as if we are something we are not. We are here just as we are!

Let me tell you, the vibe in that room completely changed. We laughed. We cried. Some ladies found a seat on the floor, created small groups, and settled in all cozy together. It was beyond beautiful. Walls of comparison, aloneness, and perfectionism broke apart that day because I was willing to go first.

So, imagine with me right now. My shoes are off, my face is bare, and I am coming to you exactly as God created. Cozy in my jammies, a glass of wine in hand, I'm admitting to you I am just a girl who said yes to God. He wrote a story so beyond what I could have imagined, I find myself driven to invite you into it. I won't have all the right answers. I may even say things other Christians thought or wrestled with, but never felt accepted saying.

We will cry together. We will laugh a bit. More importantly, this unexpected story will challenge you. It may even rock you to your core, as it did me. As you wrestle with truth, and it stirs your soul, may you remember I am sitting right here, barefoot with you, just a girl. So, my first question to you is this. Do you believe God has an adventure for you to say yes to?

Even more so, *will* you say yes, believing He will be with you, carrying, providing for, and transforming you along the way? If I can say yes to God, so can you.

Now that we're comfortable, like girls at a slumber party, there are three things you must know.

First, I never dreamed of being a mom. I now know that doesn't make me a terrible mother. It's just a part of my story. I am not naturally nurturing. For real, the first diaper I ever changed was my first-born son. I did it completely wrong and wept the entire time. Let's just say I rode a steep learning curve being a new mom at twenty-one years old. So, for you my friend, you don't have to be good at something to say yes.

Second, my husband Cory is hands down the funniest human on this earth. Somehow, even amid chaos and pain, he makes fun an important part of our home. I know that has nothing to do with us or you, but this piece of information may provide insight as you read some pages ahead. He is our rock. I'm here to remind you it is okay to laugh.

Finally, I am just a small-town girl, adventuring my way through life, saying yes to all God has for me. I am the underdog, completely confident big and beautiful adventures lie ahead of me. As I look into this world where everyone holds up their filtered pictures for the universe to see—seeking approval of themselves and their beauty—I feel compelled to say the freedom that comes from allowing the world to see all of you, as the person God made you to be, is more freeing and braver than pretending your way through. Your story may be different. Perhaps you graduated from law school with honors and are saving babies. I celebrate you. We sure need people like you in this world. No matter your accomplishments, or how you feel about them, I am here to tell you that you are extraordinary—not because of what you can do or have done, but because of what God can do through you if you let Him.

With eternity in its proper perspective, we all come to the table equally human but intricately designed and called upon for superhuman work. Why? Because God loves to give us more than we can handle. That's right. I know that seems backward from what we hear as we grow up, and not at all reassuring. Let me affirm you. When God calls you outside of what you are good at—asked to walk on water when you can't even swim, or told you're going to be a foster parent and you're not even sure you like kids—that is when He puts on the superhero cape and does the saving we can't. Be encouraged. If you feel average, if you don't have a seminary degree and you aren't even sure who God is in your life, He still has a plan and purpose for you. All you need to do is ask Him. Invite Him into your day, sit back, and let the adventure begin. If you aren't on the edge of your seat riding out the adventure God designed for you, maybe instead of inviting God along with you, you need to accept His invitation to go along with Him. Be ready. When He asks you to say yes to something impossible, remember He made you for this. You are not alone. You are not to wear the cape. God is. It's time we remove our fancy shoes, stop encouraging people to see us, and instead move out of the way so they can see Him.

My hope is for you to sense a bond of friendship as I share my story of vulnerable obedience. I pray with each letter and word that your own story intertwines with the journey on which God took my heart. As a daughter of utmost King, may these letters and this story stir in your soul a desire to press into your own eternal adoption.

As we sit here together, my heart and soul completely exposed upon these pages, please remember I am just a girl asking another to be as just as honest. You may never become a foster parent. You may already be an adoptive parent. You, like so many of my friends, may just love a good love story. Let me encourage you. Wherever you are in your life, this story is for you. When only a superhero can save what is lost, every heart can find familiarity in the story being written.

Dear sister, take off your shoes, get cozy, and let me share with you what I know of a true superhero—and it isn't you or me.

Chapter One

The Yes: Obedience

Dear Sister,

These are my first words written to you. These letters to you are the vulnerable and honest words I am too fearful to say out loud. The truth is, I wanted to say yes to the journey toward you, but I was the one holding us back. I did not know my lack of obedience could keep me from one of the greatest gifts God had for me—YOU! May you know my hesitant yes toward the journey of foster care had nothing to do with you and everything to do with me. Learn from me, my girl, that some of the greatest gifts God has waiting for you

*will be some of your hardest yeses. Our obedi-
ent yeses to the Father guide us gently to our
truest identity, being God's beloved.*

*You are not only my child, but the child of
Christ, and it is in the blessings of your eternal heritage you will find who you are. As you
read these words, remember my earthly love
for you does not come close to the love of our
Heavenly Father. When your eyes want to
look for a sense of belonging here on Earth,
remember God's proclamations of who you
are and never forget to whom you belong.*

*My heart ached to hold you for the first
time, but my head told me I wasn't strong
enough. The list of things that held me back
from feeling confident in my abilities to
love, endure, and fight for you was far too
long. Baby, doubt held a piece of my heart
God needed to mend. My shortcomings and
doubts about myself bled into your story.*

*The start of our love story together gently
pushed me out of the boat as Jesus asked me
to come to Him over scary waters. Walking on
water was the work of a superhero. He knew I
would not be the hero I felt I needed to be for
you. He already wore the cape. Only God held
the power to save, not me!*

As you forge your way through this scary world, remember this lesson. This world, apart from Jesus, will always leave you with missing pieces and a sense of emptiness. Find your belonging in The One who is ever faithful. May these words, and those on the pages ahead, lead you to a place of worship to your Heavenly Father as they have done for me. May you see how you have been so intentionally chosen and seen. Your story will sing out to the world of His continual faithfulness!

Beloved, know that you are so loved.

Teach me to do your will, for you are my God; may your good Spirit lead me on level ground.

(Ps. 143:10)

The "Idea"

The moment he uttered the words, I shut him down so fast it was as if I shoved them right back into his mouth. No amount of woo or sweet talk could get me to hurdle over the impossible words my husband was speaking.

"Absolutely not! You will not be asking me to do more, be more, give more, and for what—to become less to the ones I'm already struggling with?" I said.

If my uncharacteristic response rocked Cory with doubt at all, he didn't let on. My husband, in all his charm, approached

me with this "idea" multiple times. He is a passionate vision-
ary, a wooer of all wooers, an enthusiast with the ability to
win over pretty much anyone with his incredible humor and
dashing good looks. Yep, he's a charmer—and the reason I
am doomed to failure when I try telling him no to anything.

Then there he stood, presenting this idea. With zero hesitation, I dug in deep and clung to my no. How could I not?
This idea came with massive, life-altering, career-shifting,
changes. A yes seemed to lead to the impossible and set me
up for complete failure. No. No. No.

Then it came—the weight. This "good person" weight I
seemed to always carry felt heavier than usual. Though sometimes I felt as if something constantly followed me, or rather,
this burden sat perched on my shoulders whispering in my
ear, convincing me I was not enough.

Have you ever felt the guilt of wanting to do the right
thing, be a good person, carry the cross? You know what I
mean, right?

Guilt weighed heavier each time I shot down my husband's idea. When I blocked my husband's words and
attempted to shut him up, I felt as if the Lord drew in closer,
whispering to me.

Cadey, you're trying to shut ME up.

I wondered. Could God and my husband be on the same
page—in agreement on this terrifying agenda?

Foster care. Each time Cory said those words, I responded
the same way.

"Absolutely not!"

However, every single time I shot back with those two words, I teetered the line of selfishness and insecurities. I'll be honest. I knew this, but didn't care. Looking purely at myself, I made my decision on the matter.

I offered the plea, "Is it so wrong to tell you and to tell God I CANNOT DO MORE? This would be too much!"

So much flowed through my mind. Was God asking me to do His work because He couldn't? Didn't He see my exhaustion from doing so much already? Surely, He knew I would probably fail. God wasn't asking me to climb Mount Everest without a harness or rope. No. This was way scarier.

I battled with excuses, and my thoughts ran wild.

It's too risky. There is too much at stake. There are many people more capable of superhero work—not me, not this. What will happen to my kids? What will happen to the life I have now?

Within these ongoing thought-battles, I began believing God was setting me up for failure. It felt like a no-win situation. In saying no to foster parenting, I felt like a weak Christian woman. In saying yes to foster parenting, I felt certain I would fail as I escorted our three children straight into a dark and scary part of this world.

I knew nothing personally of this part of the world. But I instinctively knew enough to keep away from it and to work fiercely to protect the innocence of my children. I knew this world would take us to pains' front door and promised us all loss and grief.

Finding reasons to say no continued to prove easy. While I could get over seeming weak, the scary unknowns of foster care were a different story. This world promises temporary change but leaves behind lifelong pain. I found another problem with the grand idea God planted firmly in my husband's heart—the temporary placement of a stranger's child in my home. It seemed impossible to wrap my head around. What followed that? Adoption? That meant my family would forever change. I liked it just the way it was—just the five of us. I mean, caring for three kids under six years of age seemed difficult enough to juggle, let alone love!

> *We live in a world where human beings, left to themselves, not only choose the wrong direction, but remain cheerfully confident that it is in fact the right one. (N.T. Wright)*[2]

God was pointing me in the direction He had already paved for me, and left alone to myself, I would have gladly chosen the wrong direction.

Turning My No Into A Yes

Ever notice how God sends just the right people with just the right message to bring us to just the right place of obedience?

Sometimes it's gentle, but sometimes it feels like a slap on the back of the head or a sucker punch in the gut. Let's just say God got my attention.

During this time of inner debate and wrestling with the Lord, our friend Jeff and his family came for a seasonal visit. Cory and I sat with him at the kitchen table, sharing stories and catching up with all the happenings of our families. Then Jeff said two words that sucked the air right out of my lungs.

Foster. Care.

He began sharing about receiving the foster care placement of a little girl they would soon adopt.

STOP!

How did this topic surface again—and from such an unexpected source? I could not escape it.

In half a second, the shock flamed. I grew half furious as this topic kept resurfacing while the other half trembled. At that moment, I knew—this was no joke.

Through the tears spilling from my eyes, I caught the shocked and confused look on my husband's face. Though I became quite skilled at blocking Cory's attempt to discuss the subject, the blogs and stories God skillfully maneuvered into my reading plans had already shaken me to my core. Despite that, I shamefully continued to ignore God's prompting. I even kept this from my husband. Instead of sharing, I kept it bottled inside because hiding my feelings felt safer than exposing what terrified me—until that moment.

First, I poured out my excuses.

I rattled off my crazy schedule, painting a verbal picture of the organized chaos of my week. Between parenting three young and very active children, cooking, cleaning, and assisting in ministry, I questioned how God could call me to become a foster parent. Yet, as desperate as I felt to escape it, the subject followed me everywhere.

Jeff and Cory listened with patience as I explain all my fears and expected failure. I offered reasons God must have chosen the wrong girl. I certainly didn't believe I was capable.

Without hesitation, Jeff looked at me and said, "Well Cadey, it seems like you just need to be obedient."

I tell you in a flash I slapped him and ushered him to the door—well, in my mind, anyway. I could not, nor would I have ever done that, but those were the most brutally honest and life-altering words I had ever heard. They made me angry from the blunt honesty. They also convicted me and cut deep into my soul.

How could I have forgotten my surrendered life to the Lord? I had completely shut my ears to His calling voice. Ugh.

The moment His call turned scary, I bailed. I worked myself up with worry and completely forgot the character of the God asking for all of me—not just some of me, not just specific pieces of me, but all of me. Flaws. Fears. ALL.

Do this or you are being disobedient.

God's message reached me as clearly as if it had been spoken aloud.

Gulp.

Nothing reveals the cracks in one's faith quite like God asking things that seem impossible. When God asks us to do something, doing anything to the contrary is disobedience. Trust me, those unbelievable journeys down roads untraveled towards obedience are when we see the true character of God and build muscles of character in ourselves.

That truth is so clear now, but then, I didn't understand God wasn't asking for *more* of me. He was asking for *all* of me. He already saw the selfishness and disbelief in my heart. It was in Him asking for my yes to something scary that cast light on what lurked in the shadows of my heart. Let me tell you, what I found there knocked me off my feet, and doubt spilled all over my faith. Was I such a coward in my faith to hide when things turned frightening? I always believed I was a fighter—a warrior of sorts for truth and righteousness. How was it that in all the knowledge of God—all the Bible stories I'd heard as a kid, all the times I had already experienced His faithfulness—didn't sustain my faith? I knew of God's faithfulness, yet it didn't stop my doubt. I felt weak. I felt betrayed by "self." How would God use this woman of weak faith for the work of superheroes so desperately needed in this world?

The negotiating began.

Alright God, I'll do this, but can we do it pain-free?

Silence.

Ok God, we are moving forward with certification. Can you at least promise me my kids won't get hurt?

Silence.

Well, I saw you move mountains to get us to this point, though my heart doesn't feel ready. Can you change my heart before she comes?

Silence.

Will I be enough for a hurting child? Will it be too much? Can you not give us more than we can handle?

Still, God was silent.

Each time doubt seeped into my heart, I reminded myself of God's very direct and almost audible words to me.

Do this or you are being disobedient.

Of course, God's strategic silence forced me to build muscles of faith in areas of undiscovered weakness. When His silence kept me awake at night, I defaulted to the only other thing I knew from attending Awana[3] meetings as a child. I read and searched my Bible for answers because my mind failed to feed them to me. Almost daily, I searched the Scriptures for promises God wouldn't place more on me than I could handle. I needed promises God would not allow me to fail. You know what? I couldn't find any.

Each passage I tried to manipulate into truth for me and our new journey continued to tell a different story—one I didn't want to hear. Here's what I found. Yes, God can and will give us more than we can handle. Why? He delights in being the superhero—not me, not you, not any earthly thing can do what He asks of us. He wants to bring us to our knees and shine a light on the hidden parts of our hearts because *hidden* things cannot become *surrendered* things. A lot of hidden things in my heart kept me from living fully surrendered to God's calling for my life—a calling too weighty to carry without Him doing the heavy lifting.

Sister, Sister

The day came to meet Sister. *Sister*. The nickname flowed so effortlessly from my mouth the first day we met her, and so it stuck.

The privilege of our first arranged meeting took place at the home where Sister was placed. Already, God performed so many miracles for this day to happen. Still, I felt uncertainty. While my shaky faith continued, God always leveled the ground for me. We knew little about Sister other than she was one month from turning two years old and had the hair of a lion. From her pictures, I noticed her eyes mirrored mine. She appeared doll-like, almost as if she wore make-up. We knew nothing else.

My mind raced with so many questions and my head filled with more what-ifs. While attending training classes to become a certified foster parent, we were told early, "Don't get your hopes up and DON'T expect answers." That's a tall order for an unscarred, new foster mom frightened by the thought of being a foster parent, much less the reality of it.

As we drove to an unknown neighborhood, more inner lies flooded me. This added doubt to the number of reasons I felt headed for failure at this new "job." It's sad to me now that I looked at fostering as a job. I compartmentalized the realities of falling in love with a child who wasn't mine to protect my heart. Looking at it as a task—a job—kept my heart out of it. Caring for a child alongside my own, but without my heart in it, felt impossible and robotic. But this was the plan.

Lord, can I show love to a child without falling in love with that child?

Silence.

Or do I fall madly in love, knowing what it can do for her?

Tears ran down my cheeks as I silently begged the Lord for the right love, and I begged for time—time I didn't have in my day but knew she was going to need. My heart seemed to be divided. On one side, all I wanted was enough love to give—a love she needed—a healing love of which I knew nothing. On the other, all I wanted was to protect myself and my family from heartbreak. I wasn't seeing an option to do both.

I knew so little about child trauma or the process of attachment. How does one love so big and so selflessly without knowing the details of who they are or from where they came? This question haunted my secret conversations with God.

Remember Cadey, don't get your hopes up and expect nothing.

Almost there.

I prepared to build a bridge to a little girl I would soon meet. I knew practically nothing about her except that she needed me to say yes to her. Yes, she needed a home, but her heart needed so much more.

No More Waiting

As we pulled up to the house, I turned and looked at my husband for reassurance. I needed to know we were making the right decision, that we could do this. Normally, I love a good pep talk to get me moving, but this time, I needed a miracle to get me out of the car.

I took a deep breath and stepped out.

We walked up the long driveway to the door and knocked.

I heard the patter of little feet. The knob jiggled, turned, and the door cracked open. Immediately, I mentally filed away my first observations about Sister. Determined. I surprised myself as I ached for just a moment—I wanted to learn more.

The tiniest body poked its way around the door. Hair first, followed by a great big smile. With the bluest of eyes looking straight into mine, we heard, "Oh, hi!" She welcomed us as if we were old friends.

Sister's first lesson to me came that very moment. I stood at her doorstep, shaken by doubt, yet she stepped out in complete bravery. Bravery was a battle wound she fought her entire little life. I saw it written all over her as she stood there with her shoulders back, locking eyes with me. She was breathtakingly beautiful, even at her tiny age, and she had the sassiest personality to make her the perfect portion of sweet and spicy!

I don't believe in instant love. I believe in working toward love. I do not believe in love at first sight, but I believe in what happened that night between my heart and hers. From those first two words, I knew my love for her was going to carry her—not because of me, but because that night God flooded my heart with so much love for this little girl, words can hardly define it. It wasn't a perfect love. It wasn't the love a mother feels the first time she holds her newborn. It wasn't like the love that grows for someone over many years. It was a foreign love I'd never known existed. It was a supernatural provision from God holding tight to me.

At that moment, I felt myself move out of the way. I had to. I was the one in the way of God's story for her. My desire to be the hero was minimizing the perfect provision God wanted to fill within *me* as I said yes to His plan. He didn't need me to save Sister. He was blessing me with the greatest yes of my life. Something I thought so deadly to my soul and my story began shaping into the very thing to bring me new life in Him.

This Risk

> If we are to take risks, to be free, in the air, in life, we have to know there's a catcher. We have to know that when we come down from it all, we're going to be caught, we're going to be safe. The great hero is the least visible. Trust the catcher. (Henri Nouwen)[4]

Could it be the yeses God has for you will come with risk?

This risk may be vulnerability, allowing those around you to see your imperfections.

This risk may be to go into the mission field.

This risk may be to forgive the unforgivable.

This risk may be to love the one who's hurt you most.

This risk may be the hero's work you feel too weak to do.

What if we stopped manipulating the call God has on our lives and just started saying yes with no hesitation?

Yes, I'll feed the homeless.

Yes, I'll sacrifice my comfort for the comfort of someone else.

Yes, I'll go on that mission trip.

Yes, I'll say the hard but loving thing.

> *Too often, the hesitation of figuring out if God is calling me to be obedient to something leads to missing out on my one true calling—being fully surrendered to Him. A fully surrendered heart to Jesus never questions whether their calling is to love, serve, or sacrifice for another.*

What's holding you back and creating hesitation for you?

Shame?

Imperfections?

Strongholds?

Weakness?

Could it be this whole time, as we stared at the imperfection in the mirror, we missed Jesus' perfect reflection? Far too often, I assumed my efforts created the leveling in my life. I thought I needed to fix a few things about myself before I tackled the hero's work. In reality, all I needed was a teachable, surrendered Spirit before God. I needed to recognize God's truth about myself to silence the lies that locked my lips and prevented me from saying yes.

God never asked for a perfect heart, only a surrendered one. What if we removed the superhero facade—stopped believing we need to be what we assume everyone expects us to be—to live our best life? What if we threw away that facade like the dirty rag it is? What if we started believing in the power of God's strength and faithfulness—the One already wearing the cape?

What a beautiful story for God Himself to build a bridge toward us, to desire a relationship with us—and to think the story began with Him choosing us. Wow. Even when you know God has chosen you for something specific, holding on to that requires choosing Him daily. We will never tap into the superpower God charges within us if we neglect the core of our identity. You. Me. We are Christ's beloved. As the Holy, perfect, all-knowing Father He is, we can trust Him to catch us!

Therefore, if anyone is in Christ, the new creation has come: The old has gone, the new is here! All this

is from God, who reconciled us to himself through Christ and gave us the ministry of reconciliation: that God was reconciling the world to himself in Christ, not counting people's sins against them. And he has committed to us the message of reconciliation. We are therefore Christ's ambassadors, as though God were making his appeal through us. We implore you on Christ's behalf: Be reconciled to God. God made him who had no sin to be sin for us, so that in him we might become the righteousness of God.

(2 Cor. 5:17–21)

Christ's choosing of me and calling me to surrender launched me into the choosing of others, of Sister. He remained silent and patiently waited as I wrestled with my identity in Him. He remained silent when I begged for love. He remained silent as He waited for me to be transformed—to uproot from my brain the "head-knowledge" about His love for me and plant it deep into my heart. All the knowledge in the world still lacked enough faith-power to convince me of something only transformation would. It's not a long journey—about twelve inches from your head to heart—but the daily surrender required to get it there is the transformation God desperately desires for you and me. We find our calling within that work.

Can you imagine obedience feeling like a gift from God as He presents us as a meal for those hungry for love? Can you imagine the kind of obedience where God calls us into a situation of bravery that forces us to walk on water and scream for His power? What if choosing Christ meant choosing pain, trauma, self-doubt, or a love unknown to us? Think about this for a moment. God's choosing of us included all of that. He made a choice to enter the darkness of this world, including pain, trauma, even self-doubt. (See Matt. 26:36–45.) We emulate what the superhero Himself has already performed— the saving of our lives! Perhaps now you understand. Christ, by example, gave us the perfect love story to work toward with others.

> **For God so loved the world that he gave his one and only Son, that whoever believes in him shall not perish but have eternal life. For God did not send his Son into the world to condemn the world, but to save the world through him.**
>
> *(John 3:16–17)*

Sister entered our lives when my faith threatened to break at its weakest point. Little did we know, God was calling us toward long suffering. Sister's first lesson to me of bravery proved only the beginning of my heart taking on new things. Transformation of the heart often involves far more than a one-time experience. This was true for Sister and me. The journey is rough. I cannot promise your emotions will remain intact as I strip bare the real and raw realities of foster care, homelessness, anxiety, judgments, trauma, and transformed hearts. You may even pick up a few spiritual bruises along the way, but I ask you to trust God through the process.

With outstretched, very weak arms and often doubt on my lips, I choose to say yes. Trust me, if I can say yes, so can you!

So, the journey begins.

Chapter Two

"MommyDaddy": Identity

Dear Sister,

You ask a lot of questions about who people are. You want to know every detail about where each person in your life fits, and boy is it hard to win you over. I've never thought so much about identity and how awful it would be to live without answers, even more so as a child. Without a solid foundation in your iden- tity, everything about you feels broken.

God gave me the vision of what He does for us through you. As I hold your hand in every question and confusion, I continue to beg the Lord to whisper promises of owner-

ship to you in His Fatherly way. Only He can provide for you an unshakeable identity—one that comes without change because of our earthly circumstances or choices. As I beg our Heavenly Father to answer the questions for you about who you are, I can see Him changing the answers in myself of who I know as myself. As I pray blessings over you at night, I can feel them boomerang back onto me. "You are the daughter of the King. There is absolutely nothing you can do to change that."

Sister, don't expect an imperfect world to love you utterly because it will surely hand you an identity that your soul longs for, eternally. So as we wait for Heaven, know He isn't waiting to be with you. He is with you now. He is your Father now, desiring to walk in step with you now.

The LORD is my shepherd, I lack nothing. He makes me lie down in green pastures, he leads me beside quiet waters, he refreshes my soul. He guides me along the right paths for his name's sake. Even though I walk through the darkest valley, I will fear no evil, for you are with me; your rod and your staff, they comfort me. You prepare a table before me in the presence of my enemies. You anoint my head with oil; my cup overflows. Surely your goodness and love will follow me all the days of my life, and I will dwell in the house of the LORD forever.

(Ps. 23)

It's awkward, you know. You expect a child coming as you prepare to do what a parent does, without gaining the parent title. You may feel the most profound love a parent feels, yet one foot is out the door. You may see injustices and want to fight like a parent would, from hell to high water, but you aren't invited to do that. You may love, and they may hate.

This is being a foster parent.

You hope they will love you back, but you also don't want to take anyone else's place in their heart. You prepare the home. You buy them things not knowing what they prefer. You invite social worker after social worker into your home to inspect, pick through your finances, undergo background checks, and examine your family habits.

This is what God called us into.

Becoming a foster parent doesn't hold the same exciting anticipation as many other parenting journeys. As a foster parent, you know that specific day is a nightmare reality for that child and their family. Some children are only hours from being traumatically ripped from their loved ones before being placed in your foreign arms. Are you supposed to be excited or heartbroken?

This is the painful and awkward reality of foster parenting.

To do the back-breaking work of being a foster parent with no promotional title of Mom or Dad, and no mentioned "happily ever after," takes transformational work. That doesn't happen overnight. The heart's transformation occurs when we stop looking at the journey through our eyes and instead start looking at the trip through the eyes of a broken child. The cost of this obedience omits comfort and replaces it with pain.

Foster parenting could no longer be about me. It needed to be about Sister. However, no matter how hard I tried and prepared, the fear and anxiety of the unknowns always brought me back to myself.

I believed my heart would change once I held that child in my arms. I thought I would magically want what's best for them and selflessly lay down my life for them. I thought I would no longer think about the cost to our family. Yes, every fiber in a mother's being feels this way and believes it, but I have learned a child cannot transform a heart. A child cannot break a parent from selfishness. A child doesn't title a parent. A child is a child—whether biological, foster, adoptive, or caretaker.

Every parent needs a heart surgeon of sorts. A surgeon can transform the heart to expand it and repair it when it's deformed. Transformation is God's job. Our obedience to Him leads us to this point, which is the plan. Holding the title of parent wouldn't make us enough for them, only God is enough. Selfishness needed to be removed from my heart, with the delicate precision of a skilled surgeon, for obedience to grow. Even with all the best intentions in place, I could not repair myself.

And so began the long, hard work of heart surgery.

Sister's Arrival

The day finally arrived for Sister to come "home" to us. I tried to wrap my heart around the stark contrast in emotions—one moment feeling as if we were preparing for a babysitting gig and the next daydreaming this might be the first day of her forever new life.

Then she arrived.

She stood in the doorway with her social worker—black trash bags piled behind the two of them filled with Sister's things. I stood there, confused. None of this felt familiar to a child coming home.

Sister pushed her way past all of us standing at the door and made a beeline straight for the pile of toys I strategically placed in eyeshot, hoping to nudge her to step inside.

"Oh, WOW!" Sister said as she opened every drawer and toy box. Within minutes, the house looked as if a tornado ripped its way through the living room. We placed all her belongings in the garage and began our first day together.

I caught myself thinking we should toss those bags and just buy her all new things. In an instant, God paused me.

This is not trash, Cadey. This is not just about starting new. This is about you needing to invite in the old.

Oof.

I retrieved her things and slowly opened each trash bag. I watched as Sister inched closer and closer to me, pressed by curiosity. She smiled and picked up her favorite things. There wasn't an "Oh, WOW!" response, but there was a sense of comfort. Her bunny, jammies, and memories soon lay on the floor, piled next to the new things. I stepped back and took in the scene before me. Sister needed the new things in the original pile, but the old things made her who she was. To build a bridge of love and attachment to her, I couldn't throw away the old and rush to the new. I needed to take time to learn and understand these pieces of her. My new toys held none of the memories she clung to; they never could.

Heart repair number one: I needed to invite in all of Sister—the old and the new. Throwing away those trash bags and buying her new things—things that matched my things—would be for me, not for her. Though the idea brought me comfort, I knew at that moment I must place my ideals and comfort aside. My focus and concern must now be all about her. I would need to bend, to change, to like something I had never liked before. This was the cost, and it was breaking me.

Binding Wounds

At the beginning of most relationships, there is a time of adjustment. Discovery is new and things seem pleasant and peaceful, perfect even—the honeymoon phase. For some, it lasts a few days as people settle into a routine. For us with

Sister, the honeymoon lasted only a moment. The shock of the immediacy of such hard changes hit me instantly. Within the first 10 minutes, I felt like a stranger in my home. The house filled with a unique aroma, a different type of energy, and felt unfamiliar. Whatever I imagined in my head while waiting for this day was nothing like this. This new reality—feeling like a stranger in my home—caught me off guard. Who knew one tiny person could change so much, so fast? I knew grafting together two completely different families and worlds would not happen overnight, but this shook me hard.

Grafting is a farmer's process. It's quite magical and results in producing the most sought-after and rare fruits. A farmer takes the bud or a cut branch of one plant and places it into another plant's wounded area—a wound intentionally made to create space for new growth. The farmer then ties or binds the two plants tightly together, bandaging the damage as he fertilizes and nurses the hurt back to health. Over time, the two plants grow as one. The most beautiful part, because two plants now growing together as one, is that the fruit produced from the grafted branch is new. The only way grafting happens is by wounding. Without cutting the base plant open, the separated bud or branch cannot grow within it.

Deep within, I knew my heart needed to experience wounding to create a space for Sister. Painful? Yes. Time and patience—an abundance of both—were necessary for the grafting to heal and bring our hearts together. The process would feel foreign, but over time, bring us together as one.

A Little Runner

Less than twenty-four hours in our home, Sister tried to run away. To my astonishment, I learned it was not her first attempt at such a bold move, nor would it be her last. How does one graft together with someone who doesn't want to stick around? Little did I know we were still in the throes of the wounding process. The time for grafting was still far off.

Somehow, this tiny but mighty toddling bundle of business heaved open the hefty front door, as if to break out of prison, and dashed up the driveway without looking back. Thank goodness the loud creak of the front door served as a signal to anyone within earshot that she was running again. The family would jokingly call out, "We've got a runner!" This meant Sister was halfway up the driveway. Before we learned it would take five tricky locks to keep Sister safely inside, we experienced many sprints up the drive. Each time, she waddled her way as fast as her little legs would go—until I caught up to her and snatched her up in my arms. She wailed. Kicked. Bit. She threw her head back to cause me to struggle to hold her. Just the touch of me made her upset. And you know what? I got it. The longing for home would make anyone run.

She

Sister would point at me and say, "She (referring to me) banana?" Translation: Sister wanted me to give her a banana, but she didn't know what to call me, so she called me, "She."

This was the beginning of our relationship. Anyone can be She: the neighbor, the lady scooping ice cream, the stranger down the street. I fell into that category. She, the lady that gets me what I need. I tried to teach her at least, "Cadey. You can call me Cadey."

Nope! I was She.

It's a frustrating title to hold when all you want is to fast-forward to friend, or even better, Mom. Every day I saw Sister desperate to come out of isolation, but she just wasn't ready.

In these moments, instead of feeling the devastation of rejection I expected to feel, I felt only turmoil for her. My heart broke, wounded for her rather than from her rejection of me. Rejection can be an impossible hurdle to clear in the pursuit of love. Rejection was the only love language Sister knew how to speak, so our love had to start from those wounds.

No volume of presents, toys, McDonald's Happy Meals, or caretaking would convince Sister she was safe and loved at home with us. It was going to take all of that, plus time. Her new identity with us confused and irritated her. Things that seemed insignificant to us rubbed her the wrong way—like a scratchy blanket wrapped tightly from head to toe. She walked around like a foreigner in a strange place. When we talked to her, she looked at us as if we spoke an unfamiliar language. She self-isolated in a full house surrounded by so many things.

Watching her carry her pain all alone wounded me even more.

> *How many people have we given up a relationship with when they just needed more time? A little more work could have drawn you into the spaces of their heart where walls once stood.*

We soon learned the importance of titles to Sister. In a full room, she wanted to know every name, how they knew her, or why they were there. If you meant anything to her, she gave you a name. Our daughter, Marlie, received the honor of the first Sister-assigned nickname. LaLa. We watched Sister name each person in our lives: the neighbor, the babysitter, everyone—except for Cory and me.

MommyDaddy

One night, like most every night, Sister sat in her highchair, refusing to eat—not because she didn't like it or wasn't hungry, but more to test control. Food served as a game of control for her, and oh boy, was I losing!

The tests of control became a tense reminder of the differences and changes in our home. Gone were the old, mostly peaceful nights at the table. We now lived a new, more disruptive normal. I'm unsure if she enjoyed negative attention more than positive, but we soon understood these episodes as her way of checking in with us. In action rather than words, she was asking, "Are you still there? Would you still love me if [her particular behavior at the time]?"

Because God was working to repair my heart, I soon saw her fits and need for control differently than I would otherwise. The refusals at dinner weren't about food, but about trust. This behavior came from a place of pain—not because she was bad or ill-mannered.

This night, Sister began throwing her banana slices on the floor. I reached down and picked them up. She threw another. I picked it up—and so the game began. Each time she threw a banana slice, I picked it up. Oh, how she loved this game.

As the game continued, something changed.

"MommyDaddy!"

Astonished, Cory and I whipped our heads around and looked wide-eyed at Sister.

"MommyDaddy," she said again.

Cheers erupted. Our enthusiastic reaction only encouraged her to continue shouting it, growing a little louder each time.

Cory and I looked at each other, pointed to the other, and asked, "Are you, Mommy or Daddy?" While that may seem silly, we soon discovered to her we were both.

Both?

Yep. Sister felt no need to distinguish one from the other. MommyDaddy, our first honored title from Sister, proclaimed that she saw us as someone she needed. Oh, maybe at first she just wanted to watch me pick bananas off the floor. However, the foundations of trust had finally begun, and it was worth celebrating. Our elation mirrored a great game-day victory.

Why MommyDaddy? Sister didn't know if I was Mommy or Daddy. She also didn't need to care. The titles she awarded distinguished what each specific person did for her. All she needed to know was that those titles held importance. A new-found need for her, as she gradually grafted into the Fenn family, was being cared for—even if it was just picking up her food and feeding her.

There was little to no meaning or attachment to the name MommyDaddy. The title she chose for Cory and me had nothing to do with us and everything to do with her. She was a party of one, trying to figure out how to be a part of "us."

I graduated from She to MommyDaddy, and I could not have been more ecstatic. When Sister screamed it across the playground. Heads would turn to look, confusion on their face. She sang it in the hallways at church and told the pre-school workers it was my name. I embraced it in public, but knew it drew unwanted attention.

Sister and I were in the grocery store one afternoon, circling the cookie stand, when a woman approached us.

"Are you not her mom?"

"Excuse me?!"

"She called you MommyDaddy. Is that just a nickname or something?"

Let me pause and say something. Unfortunately, this situation happens all too often. Sometimes, out of naïve curiosity, we ask hurtful things. As an unseasoned foster mom, I lacked a much-needed one-liner to respond for such occasions. So, I bit back, "This is my foster daughter."

Her response filled me with grief and shame. Ugh. I opened the door.

"Oh, was she a drug baby? That's so scary. I could never do what you are doing."

How could I have led Sister into a moment where a stranger spoke about her identity and who she must be?

I dropped the cookies I clutched, spun my shopping cart around, and made haste away from the woman.

I felt gut-punched, my lungs tight. I gasped for a breath. Sister, seated in the cart facing me, stayed silent. I had no words. Sister and I avoided eye contact throughout the rest of the store.

As I pushed her to the car, every emotion swept over me. Anger. Sadness. Rage. Shame. I fought a battle of thoughts.

What was that woman thinking? Could she not see Sister sitting right there, listening to her every word?

I cannot imagine how sad that must make her—to hear those things from a stranger.

I mean, I know she was speaking out of ignorance, but who just says that out loud?

How could I have introduced her with that title? She has a name!

As I buckled Sister into the backseat of the car, I heard the Lord whisper.

Beloved.

Beloved: Child of God

I believe we all hold the responsibility of ushering friends, spouses, family, and even strangers into a beloved title.

Heart repair number two: The way I see others needs to be how God sees them.

The child who lost her family to drugs and alcohol—beloved.

The Mom who struggles with addiction and neglectful behavior—beloved.

The privileged woman walking through the store ignorantly asking questions—beloved.

The caretaker holding broken hearts in one hand and self-doubt in the other—beloved.

Titling those around us with the name Beloved removes none of the pain or trauma of their lives. More so, it clarifies who they are to God, not what acts they've committed, nor any horror they've experienced. As we stand at God's doorway, trash bags in hand, He takes all of us with a purpose to create something new! With this heart repair, we can love anyone and graft them into our lives and families the way God has done for us.

A title holds no power. Achievement holds no love. Anyone looking at titles to find their identity will eventually decay from the emptiness deep within their soul. If we leave our identity to the shakiness of our strength and abilities, one foul twist and turn of events—losing a job, parent, child, or spouse—can leave us wondering who we are and if we matter in this world. God designed us to place our entire lives—including ourselves, our marriages, our homes, our children, our jobs, and our obedience—all in the identity of Him. We should graft ourselves deep into the brokenness of Jesus on the Cross.

The ignorant strangers around you may question your motives and abilities. You may even doubt God asked the right person to say yes to this journey, but I know one thing without a doubt. If you listen, God will whisper to you, too.

You are my beloved.

Chapter Three

The Doorway: Love

Dear Sister,

A heart set free is one that denounces that hiding is safer than being seen. A soul set free by God's hand of love and grace is one that is like a flag blowing in the wind, never in a posture of perfectly straight, but always flying high for others to see. Letting out the sails of your heart enables others to see its true colors, the definition of it, the description of its purpose, and why it needed to be seen. Letting your heart fly free is scary, I know. Your heart, already broken so many times, leaves you with scars you live with daily. Don't allow those scars to hold you back from love, from being seen by others and flying high! Your battle scars are a part of you. They do not define you. When you are hurting and overwhelmed, know that you are not alone. Pain and uncertainty are a part of setting your heart free. The ability to blow in the crazy winds of this world only happens by allowing those around you to see you in everything you are!

God's gift of grace and mercy allows you to sail in the wind without fear of blowing away, never to be seen again. God's care for you will hold you, even when life feels out of control. And God's redemption will forever redefine the darkness of your story into beauty if you let Him. Know that your heart's tenderness and the triggers that sting do not make you weak. The capability of strength you hold is in your willingness to fly freely in the winds of the Lord. The Lord will usher you toward Himself. As you stand in the doorway, nervous to take those first steps, follow His lead.

There is no fear in love. But perfect love drives out fear, because fear has to do with punishment. The one who fears is not made perfect in love. We love because he first loved us.

(1 John 4:18–19)

The Love Bank

Maybe once I have deposited enough, then she will hug me, I thought.

Every day I worked with diligence and purpose to deposit bits of trust into Sister's mind, hands, and heart. I imagined it like a piggy bank. A child from trauma needs more than their heart comforted and a bunch of promises. They need their hands filled when hungry. They need to be communicated with, not spoken over. Every move either makes a deposit of trust or makes a withdrawal and creates separation.

I found simple mom duties the most vulnerable to her because many of those activities required touching or nearness. Big love happened in the smallest moments. When I spoke to her, I noticed she only responded when I was on my knees eye to eye with her. Whether she wasn't accustomed to being spoken to or cared less about what I said didn't matter. *Seeing* Sister—meeting her where she stood—that's what mattered. Oh, how my legs ached from the constant bending and squatting to look into Sister's eyes. Sometimes I felt as if I kneeled hundreds of times a day, but my comfort mattered less than Sister's needs. When my legs felt too sore to kneel one more time, I remembered the importance of this simple act for Sister's heart.

How had I never viewed my movements in life with this depth of importance before? I soon learned the importance of my every move—the way I smiled or didn't, the tone of my voice, or the quickness of my hand coming toward her face to wipe her mouth. She watched them all—hyper-aware of me, my movements, and how to predict what I'd do next. One misspoken word would send us back to square one. Running one minute late to pick her up would throw us three steps back. One unknown trigger could prove catastrophic.

My entire life shifted from a steady, somewhat predictable, forward motion to what felt like backward and sliding sideways all at once. That constant change in direction and sense of urgency would leave anyone feeling sick. I felt it deep in the pit of my stomach—a head-spinning, motion-sickness kind of nausea. The only way to fix both the spinning and nausea was to slow down. It's not as if I could just stop and get off like a carnival ride, but I hoped we could slow things down enough to gather our bearings.

In the mundane, ordinary, quiet moments (though few), I watched Sister. I studied the outline of her body to determine her inward emotions. Her unpredictable movements offered a little sign of how the day might unfold emotionally. My observations resulted in the curiosity of what triggered her and why. I memorized her facial expressions and reactions to things. I spent hours observing and searching her to learn more. So much of her story remained a mystery. There were too many whys with no answers, and too many pains and reactions without a story attached.

This tiny stranger was sleeping in my house, and she didn't even want me.

I wanted Sister to want me—as if proof of love somehow equates to how much one desires another.

This distant feeling between us needed to dissolve. I refused to give to it or accept it. I kept trying, backing up, trying again. Little did I know then that our love story would not come from a want or a need, but from a place of choosing.

The more I tried to be what I thought she needed, the clearer it became that I wasn't.

Family relationships triggered her childhood wounds. The mothering nature in me triggered her deepest longings. Sisters on the playground triggered her most significant loss. It seemed as if our entire world exposed her losses.

How does one soften that kind of blow?

More excruciating than experiencing brokenness within oneself is watching a child bear brokenness alone. Never, in all my life, had I begged the Lord to give me exact direction on how to love someone—until Sister. I prayed for Him to ease her pain, and give her joy. I prayed for Him to guard my hands and feet as I played a guessing game with loving and providing for her.

I watched Sister weep, her anger rise, her misplaced hatred, and saw her reject love because of its hazardous nature.

Lord, how could someone so tiny already know how scary love can be?

Triggers can be anyone or anything. I happened to be Sister's biggest trigger.

Triggers are a re-lived experience of what once almost destroyed you. What does the pursuit of loving someone look like when they continually show you they don't want love, or fear it? Once I saw the depth of the darkness and pain Sister lived day in and day out, I knew helping her reach a place of healing fell beyond my reach. She wasn't even able to enjoy the joys of family. She lived in a prison of fear and pain. Nothing I could do would change that immediately. The invitation and love I held out to her proved ineffective as a bandage for a wound that deep. It only worked to expose it.

Time.

Patience.

It was at this slowed pace God taught me my place in Sister's life.

I held an unrealistic expectation for my presence in her life—and all the love I offered—to bandage her wounds and nurse her back, happy and whole. This unwelcoming pace with Sister redirected me to remember who God is and who I could never be.

God is the healer.

God is the comforter.

God is patient.

God is love.

We love because He first loved us.

(1 John 4:19)

I desired for Sister to accept from me a love riddled with confusion, selfishness, and self-doubt. The love God directed my hands and feet into giving her required my surrendered heart. I silently prayed.

Not my will, but Yours be done.

Little Bodies In The Bed

One memorable morning, I awoke to the mild chill of crisp air and the smell of pine trees drifting in from the open window above our bed. I felt the warmth of one tiny little body next to me. I knew it was my youngest son. He sleepwalks into our room nearly every night, which I don't mind and expect. He can't sleep without the touch of someone else, even if it's just our feet. As if his unconscious body memorized the way, asleep or awake, he makes his way close to me.

As I began shifting my weight ever so carefully to avoid disturbing my husband or our sleeping son, I soon realized he wasn't the only tiny little body in our bed. There were three. While the addition of three little bed hoppers wasn't unusual, once my sleepy stupor passed, a frantic feeling washed over me.

I have four! Where is the fourth?

Was she lost in the pillows or under the oversized down comforter? Where else would she be?

While Sister arrived just two months prior, those eight weeks seemed the longest of our lives—for her as well.

Bedtime rituals—once filled with hugs, snuggles, affirmations of I love you, and I love you more, kisses, then prayers—changed with Sister's arrival. We continued the routine, just different for Sister, as she wanted no part of it. From her crib, she screamed if we entered the room. When this happened, we turned and rushed back to the doorway. Standing there, we practically shouted nighttime prayers and our goodnights. Because she resisted being touched, I would give her a good-night wave, blow a kiss (for my mama's heart), and close the door. Nothing about it felt natural or nurturing. I listened to her cries from the backside of her bedroom door.

Every mom knows the distinct cries of their children, and even though Sister was still new in our home, I knew the differences in her screams and cries—cries for food, whininess, and pain. Sister's pain-filled, heart-wrenching cry every night grew greater when I drew in too close. Many nights I anguished, leaning against the door, sliding until I lay in the doorway of her room begging God to do what I couldn't.

Lord, comfort her. Be with her.

No child should ever have to comfort themselves alone.

I quietly counted her breaths and listened to how she soothed herself. I forced myself to cry without a sound so she wouldn't detect my presence. A steady flow of tears streamed down my face. I cried out to God on her behalf.

How long will this last?

What else can I do for her?

Those late nights became a vulnerable space for me as I faced the most challenging conversations with God—conversations I never knew I could have with Him. I spoke with doubt and fear. With raw honesty, I poured out my sadness amid Sister's. I grieved what my family once looked like. I missed the joy that no longer bounced off the walls. I wished for Sister to slip into our family like a missing puzzle piece, but she walked from room to room instead, alienated from us all. I cried out to God in that doorway, broken, begging for Him to meet me. It felt as if Sister's heart lay on the line, and He was the only one to save it.

Without fail, each morning Sister sat and waited in the dark, alone, never calling out. So, each morning I waited for Sister's invitation. Sometimes the wait grew to hours. I waited patiently to be there when it came—sometimes opening the door before the last words spilled from her mouth.

"MommyDaddy, out!"

The Doorway

So, snuggling in bed—the five of us—would normally make my heart feel warm and full. Instead, the moment became a painful reminder of someone missing—someone just one room over—someone I could not approach in her crib, gather up, and bring to bed with us. She refused it.

I slipped from the bed undetected and maneuvered through the dark to claim my slippers. The wood floor felt frigid from the outside air. A chilly breeze from the window, though only slightly lifted, further awakened me. I needed to check on Sister.

As I eased open the already-cracked bedroom door, there she lay, her little body curled up in the doorway. Here she slept, no blanket, curled tight for warmth, pacifier in hand. The blanket lay two feet behind her, not quite making it to her sleeping spot. I paused for a moment in disbelief. Shame settled in my chest as I imagined her night there on the floor.

I scooped up her cold little body, stealing a moment to snuggle her close as she slept—something she usually refused. I carried her to the chair, eased in, and rocked her. I wept over her, praying over every inch of her, begging God to heal it. Slowly, her eyes cracked open. Fear overtook her face—panic—like when you wake up not knowing where you are.

I invited her into our first vulnerable moment together.

"Shhh, go back to sleep," I whispered as I tucked her wayward curls behind her ear.

Never had I felt this vulnerable rocking a baby in my arms. I slowed myself to imagine what her heart must be feeling. She turned her body away from me, withdrew her hands from mine, but she stayed. Her body was tensed at first, stiffened as if to tell me how uncomfortable she felt. I continued to rock, fighting through the tension. I just kept rocking and whispering.

"You are safe. You are loved."

I must admit, her denial of me made me sad. This tense rocking felt awkward and broke my heart. As stilted as the action felt, I more so desired for her to experience love—the love I offered her. Yes, I desperately wanted her to love me in return. How could I not wish that? Denying it would omit an important truth. Can one usher another into a love story and leave their own heart out of the equation? Impossible. Inhuman. I couldn't be a robot.

I once believed denying myself—denying my heartbreak of her refusal to accept me—made everything about Sister and her healing. It's a convincing lie. In contrasting truth, God allowed the brokenness of my heart to expand and create space for her. I required that broken heart. I needed to feel it. This denial of love and affection became a key part of the journey of loving the brokenhearted. At the time, I had no idea I needed to be broken, too.

I sat there, rocked, and forced myself to feel what I imagine she felt and why she felt it. I allowed my heart to break for her, and eventually for me.

I relied on God to tell me what to do next because my nurture and my instinct were not what she needed. I only knew the very thing Sister fought was the one thing she most wanted. She worked tirelessly to make everyone around her believe she didn't need them or anything from them. When she needed something, her manipulation to get it told her story repeatedly to everyone around. Instinctively, she encased herself in so many emotional barriers, it seemed impossible to reach that little heart of hers. Even a child knows how to protect themselves from pain.

Everything I assumed and feared about foster care fell away. The fear of taking in and loving a child, only to be taken away, disappeared. This was no longer about adoption. This was no longer about forever. This was no longer about whether I would have to say goodbye tomorrow or the next. This was about seeing a child in pain and feeling that pain, too.

Once we take our agenda out of our pursuit to love others, it becomes a love story on its own. I learned the only sustainable love is one dependent on the Heavenly Father. Once I identified the selfish nature within me, it became easier to set myself aside and focus on her healing.

Then "normal" changed, just like that.

Sister's hard edges softened. She no longer stayed in the doorway, but each night inched her way closer to me. Each day I woke up, scooped her into my arms, and rocked her. With each passing day, a love story unfolded, and a heart gently healed.

One morning, I awoke when a tiny hand touched my face. Sister awkwardly stood there not knowing what to do, but I knew. I had seen that look before. Without saying a word, she was asking for an invitation. She needed something but was too afraid to ask. For whatever reason, on that day, she crossed through the doorway in full vulnerability. Her need to experience love became more significant than her fear.

I opened my arms, and she slowly climbed in. With her face outward and no touching, she laid there stiff as a board, just as when we rocked. When the darkness faded with the rising sun, I scanned the room. I spotted three little bodies curled up asleep, and Sister who was sitting up in bed looking at us.

"We are all here," she whispered.

"Yes, we are," I whispered back.

That morning, for the first time, she counted herself in the "us." For that moment, she was no longer a part of one. Experiencing love in the way God knew she needed led her to a place of healing. My love alone, for her, would have fallen short and slipped straight into selfishness.

In California, we experience crazy earthquakes. From an early age, we learn a doorway is a safe place. Even with everything crumbling around you, the doorway is the most crucial place to be. This is precisely what Sister desired, safety. She looked for what her soul longed to find. She wanted to enter a genuine relationship, to give and receive love, but needed first to know the relationship was safe. The doorway became that for her as she made her way to my arms. She could lay there, inching her way closer, looking at the life she wanted, but needing to be comfortable enough to embrace. She needed to be comfortable enough to ask.

No one can stay knocking at the doorway forever. They may not even know why they are there, asking for you. They may want the invitation from you, but won't take it. They aren't ready. They simply want to know you are there. Are you listening? Are you inviting them in, in any state, in any posture, with no agenda other than love?

Love is not always a two-way street. Love in its truest form can also be one way, moving only you in one direction toward another. This type of love does not expect affirmation from the other that their heart is safe because one-way love isn't about safety at all. It's about the other person. It's right in the middle of this type of love that motives, intentions, fears, and pains rise to the surface.

> *To be affirmed that your love is returned numbs the fears we all have about being unlovable, and gives breath to an unhealthy, unauthentic, conditional love.*

If you are obedient, you love me.

If you give me what I want, you love me.

If you respect me, you love me.

If you make me feel special, you love me.

What if the type of love you're called to give isn't determined by what someone does or doesn't do, but by what *you* do? What if the person standing in your doorway is waiting for an invitation of love, with nothing to give in return?

Can you imagine if our Heavenly Father asked us to turn to Him and love Him on His terms, His timing, emulating His perfection? I don't know about you, but I would fail every time. I would fall short in my trust and desire for Him because I am broken and selfish. He holds His arms open, and I continue to choose the doorway, standing there with mistrust and lacking faith. More often than not, we choose to sleep in the doorway of faith rather than fully experience the Father's eternal and vulnerable love. Yet, He never stops inviting us in.

Brokenness surrounds us all—pain we didn't ask for or expect. Friends, family, and neighbors may be desperate for an invitation that leads them to love. Scary? Yes. Uncomfortable? Definitely. Extending an invitation means you must make the first move. Do it. Leave the safety net. Someone needs you to say yes.

Is it your neighbor who seems lonely? Is it a distant acquaintance you see occasionally? Perhaps it's a family member or wayward child? All you may need is to look up and see who God has for you to love.

Check your expectations because the experience will be like nothing you anticipated. You may need to extend a million invitations to see one accepted. It's important to not lose heart. Remember, the broken hold a hidden story still untold. Move toward them and learn as you build your bridge to their heart. Feel your human nature and be honest about your inability to care in the way needed. Cry out to the Lord to unlock broken pieces of your heart so you may love in ways you never knew you could.

Then, walk to the doorway, scoop them up, and invite them in. Break through the awkwardness of vulnerability for them by opening your heart and sharing your brokenness. When they stiffen, demonstrate trust—not because you are always trustworthy (remember, we are human and not perfect). Being broken isn't something to fear, but choosing to be alone in this life is. When dark days linger over those around us, may we be the light in the doorway, inviting others in to experience love.

What if we rocked others in their pain so consistently, their pain became ours? What if trusted love grew by walking with others through their pain, rather than acting from a written or imagined rule or law of expected behavior?

Love is the transformative power we are all capable of possessing that truly changes lives when given.

If we do not allow ourselves to be broken for those breaking around us, our invitations toward others will never move into a transformative love.

What if God is asking us to extend the invitation, to be the initiators, so another person in our lives never feels unwanted, or like they are the recipient of an obligatory invite? Embracing this type of transformation love gives you the strength to hold tight to others who may respond to your invitation with tense pushback—those who "sleep in the doorway" out of fear only observing what's being offered and not fully accepting it. Only God can lead them to heal. You can be the arms that hold them through that journey. Be brave. Take a step.

I found the power of God's love in the doorway, and so can you.

Chapter Four

Scavenger: Provider

Dear Sister,

I work tirelessly to get you to understand that you will be taken care of. I hold your face daily and remind you I can't know what you need unless you ask, so ask, baby. I am for you, not against you! It's your reservation to ask that hurts the most. The inability to realize that you need care outside of what you can give yourself.

There is a blurred stare, a far-off world you go to when you get hungry. I have had to teach you to tell me, to listen to your body as it speaks to you, and to not hold it to your-

self, but to rely on me. I am here with you, so ask, baby.

It's funny. You are the tiniest person and a six-pack is painted on your little belly, but you can pack in some food. You won't stop until I tell you. I remind you there will be more whenever you need it. There is no need to horde or hide for later. Leave your scavenger heart, and cling to me. I have become that inner voice for you as you learn to come into this world. Now there is a bit of a co-dependency as you venture out. You are always looking over your shoulder to make sure we are in an eye-shot of one another. You lock eyes with me as we eat in restaurants or visit with friends. Your eyes say, "I trust you a bit more now."

I will never forget to provide for you. I will never lose sight of your needs. Every time I am gifted with the opportunity of providing for you, my prayer is that you see a better understanding of our Heavenly Father. As you build trust with me, may it project you into a trusting relationship with the God who numbers the stars and never forgets—the One who wrapped you in comfort before I even knew you, and the One who will never leave you nor forsake you. May your built dependency

*on my care project you into a more profound
need to lay your needs in the arms of the
Heavenly Father.*

So do not worry, saying, "What shall we eat?" or
"What shall we drink?" or "What shall we wear?"
For the pagans run after all these things, and your
heavenly Father knows that you need them.

(Matt. 6:31–32)

One. Two. Three. I counted little heads. Lackadaisically, I
kept one eye on them as they romped around the playground,
all while enjoying conversation with a friend. I slipped into
the habits I created for years as a mom. For eight years, I
allowed all three of my kids to play freely around me. I never
gave a thought they would feel neglected or afraid because I
was just eight feet away.

Gasp!

Eight feet is too far! My brain shifted into overdrive. I
now have four kids. Four kids! The shock of it all snapped me
back into my new reality. My eyes frantically searched.

I scanned the dining area of a small hamburger stand
next to the play area. There I caught the top of Sister's curly
hair weaving through the tables. As I watched her closely,
I noticed the way she held her body close, sneaking low to
the ground with a mischievous grin on her face. She slipped
quietly behind her targets, crouching behind the customers'

backs, easing her way in close behind them but careful not to touch anyone. Her lips stretched out toward a stranger's straw, which conveniently stuck out just far enough for Sister to sneak a sip. From table to table, she crept. Unfazed and relatively confident, like this was a common occurrence for her. Shocked and rather grossed out, I rushed over to her, completely embarrassed even though she remained undetected.

"Sister, I can get you a drink if you are thirsty."

"No! I ok."

She pushed me away, bouncing from table to table, making sure I saw she was no longer sneaking sips from strangers' drinks. She slipped out of my hands so quickly I almost missed the glance that taught me something significant about pain. Sister's coy grin and bouncing hair could not mask the anguish in her eyes.

From my childhood, I associated skipping with joy. I remember holding hands with my best friend at six years old, giggling, whispering, smiling, and skipping along. As the sun beamed in our hair, we talked about simple things, and played make-believe. Our biggest fear was daylight turning to dusk, which meant only one thing—playtime ended for the day. As every child should have, ours was a life of innocence and ease.

Then I saw Sister skip away, alone, trying to hide the pain behind her eyes—physically acting child-like, but internally soldiering on as if preparing for another war.

I hadn't yet learned Sister needed to feel safe in every environment, whether new or old. I ignorantly went about with the natural sense of believing since I was a safe person, she should feel safe. Sister needed care, comfort, and affirmation of safety at all times. The most basic needs, like getting a drink because she was thirsty or because everyone else had one, were called into question minute by minute. Every moment I ignorantly said nothing, missing her need for reassurance, a chaos of fear grew within her.

Fear creates a scavenger's mentality—to do whatever it takes to survive.

Scavengers scrounge for any substance that will benefit them. They often fall ill from the decay they force-fed themselves—not thinking straight enough to realize their actions cause more harm than good. From garbage to junk, their minds look past the natural response of disgust from feeding off the scraps of another and instead see it as a method of survival. Fear transfers past trauma into present circumstances, causing the past to seep into the here and now.

With or without the trauma present, it lingers there to surface at unexpected times. For Sister, being surrounded by strangers all eating and drinking while her hands were empty, catastrophically launched her into survival mode.

This reminds me of the raccoons on our family farm where I grew up. I spent hours sitting in the dark garage with my hand out, holding a piece of fresh bread from the kitchen, whistling to the coons that built a home in the rafters. I convinced myself they were starving. Each morning, as I took out the trash, a multitude of little glowing eyes beamed at me as I approached the dumpster. No matter how slowly I approached or how softly I spoke, they always scurried away. Despite their flee, I just knew they wanted that yummy, warm, soft, straight-from-the-oven-and-untouched bread! I used every skill I possessed as an eight-year-old to coax the little critters down. My patience at that age spanned all of a minute or three most of the time, so it didn't take long to grow tired of trying to win them over.

Friends, how often have we given up on someone near us because they skipped away, pushed us away, or walked away only to catch a split-second glance of the pain in their eyes? Caring for those around us scavenging to feel safe and seen won't happen with just one act of provision—maybe not even two. Caring for someone—someone with pain stuffed so deep inside them you can't understand it—will not happen without you first being transformed. An eight-year-old girl doesn't have the patience, let alone the skill, to know how to feed and care for a wild animal. That takes years of time and attention to learn. Caring for the survivors of this world should place an ache in our hearts that hurts beyond a short-term encounter. It should etch its way into our hearts, redesigning its purpose and cares.

Burned Toast

One particular Sunday morning, eager for my cup of coffee to hit my veins, I sniffed a whiff. My eyes flew open the moment it hit me. SMOKE! My feet found a gear that should be sinful on Sundays. I hurdled the gate at the base of the stairs. By the time my bare feet hit the cold tile, my eyes burned from the billowing smoke coming from one corner of the kitchen. I found Sister on top of the counter, unconcerned with the rolling smoke.

In independent Sister fashion, she moved pieces of furniture that enabled her to climb onto the countertop, found the hidden key to the pantry, and proceeded to make herself some toast—attempted, anyway. (Yes, we had good reason to lock the pantry door—this being a prime example.)

Soon after, every door with valuables, or that lead outside, sported two or three locks high enough to require me to stand on my tiptoes to reach. Though, I confess, that's not saying much. I'm all of five-two with shoes. However, we believed them to be well-positioned at the time. We put everything in complete lockdown because sometimes Sister's fear caused her to run or act out. At some point, while I remained completely unaware, she saw me put the key away and plotted a plan to make toast in the morning, all on her own. Let me tell you, raising a child with insane street smarts can get a little scary.

On this particular morning, I imagined her slipping through the house on her tiptoes, sneaking past my bedroom (where I keep my door cracked and one eye open), climbing her tiny body over the baby gate (which I use as a speed bump just to slow her down). Where then, she moved heavy furniture to find the hidden key she used—correctly, I might add—to reach her golden target. Bread!

Let's pause and for me share this funny thing—an important detail. At this point in the story, you may think, well, she was hungry. That is a reasonable deduction, but an inaccurate one. Just a few feet from this horrific break-in sits a bottom drawer just for her—labeled with her name—stocked with food. Sister may take anything from it to eat, play with, or hide for later—whatever she chooses—all in her full control. The contents of that drawer belong to her.

Once she gained entry to the pantry, she got the bread, a favorite of hers. Grabbing the entire loaf (because who knows, she may need to eat all of it) she walked across the countertop over to the toaster. She must have figured out how to plug it in. (I know, terrifying, right?!) So, she toasted her bread. It popped up, but she discovered it was too hot to grab. She worked too hard for those two slices of bread, so she decided she must find a way to get them out.

NAPKINS!

Napkins always work when things are hot, right? By now, you probably have vivid images of what a napkin does when it contacts the hot insides of a recently used toaster. If I am honest, I don't like using a toaster. I am more of a broiler kind of gal. It's a good thing Sister went for the toaster instead of the broiler. Yikes! Fortunately, I found her before the smoke turned into flames—all that practice baby gate hurdling paid off!

Oh, and you wouldn't believe the first thing she asked me once I got the situation under control.

"Can I eat my bread now?"

Sigh.

You guys, all she had to do was ask. My heart broke. I find joy in providing for her because I know how much it means to her healing. What could I have possibly done for her to not trust that about me? The hurt built. I felt anger wanting to spill out of my mouth.

This is not about you.

I caught myself. It's not about me. Her behavior is a product of her pain. She is acting like a scavenger because she is afraid.

This is not a reflection of you or what you haven't done.

I spoke those words of truth over myself before I allowed anything to come out of my mouth.

Sister's fear blocked her view of seeing the provision of those around her—specifically, ME. It is my job to care for her, to provide for her. Intimacy and attachment grow between us when she allows me to be her provider. Fear breaks that. It separates her from me. Fear isolated her into believing she was safer to depend upon and provide for herself.

I called her over and gently took her face in my hands.

"Baby, why didn't you just wake me and ask for toast?"

"I wanted toast, and I didn't want to wait."

Now, let's give her some credit here. At least the girl was honest, right?

"Well, baby, you have an entire drawer of food just for you. Is that not enough?"

"I was afraid you would say no."

"But Sister, because you didn't come to me, you endangered yourself. You could have gotten so hurt."

How many times have we said that to the Lord? "God, I don't want what you have already given me because I don't trust it to be what's best. I want this!"

Or maybe we said, "God, I wasn't sure if you were going to provide, so I went for it on my own."

How many times do we settle for burned toast when God is holding out mana straight from Heaven? That's a complete analogy, my friends, but how true is that? We see what we want and what we need, but instead of trusting God as our Father, we sneak, climb, push, and fight for what we want, when we want it. We behave like scavengers, frantically fighting for survival rather than the adopted child we are. We tend to live in fear and distrust of God, leaving us further isolated from Him. God never intended for survival to be placed in our own hands. It has always been in His.

It isn't my job to take away Sister's trauma and pain. As much as I would like to believe being the best possible mom and provider would replace the scars she carries, it never will. As much as I would give my life to ease her pain, my job is to comfort her. Forcing her trauma to disappear, or believing she doesn't experience it simply because she may not remember it, would be a misguided comfort for me. Wishing away what has made her who she is, and who she will become because of it, is selfish. If I believe her trauma no longer exists because somehow I have miraculously repaired it, then I believe a lie that further isolates her.

Friends, this concept is also true with our Heavenly Father. Though He can, though He may, His job as our Father isn't to take our trauma and pain away. His job as our Father is to be *with* us in it, and through it, to comfort us in ways only He can—to provide peace in supernatural ways. It's only natural for us to believe true love would want to shield us from all the sin and garbage of this world, but God did something better. He knew healing us or shielding us from pain isn't enough. Being *with* us—now that's more than sufficient!

> **You make known to me the path of life; you will fill me with joy in your presence, with eternal pleasures at your right hand.**
>
> *(Ps. 16:11)*

God knew fullness would not be found in a pain-free life. Fullness is found in His presence alone. A survivor no longer needs to survive when they experience fullness.

Christ didn't die on the Cross that we may become animal-like in providing for ourselves—sneaking around, fighting for what we want, when we want it. No. God provided His own son to bridge the world to eternity with Him.

God designed us with a vulnerable dependability upon Him. His provision will supersede what our earthly eyes or strength can provide.

I often fight for burned toast rather than the blessings of the Father. My eyes can only see the earthly things in front of me in my smallness, and I quickly forget the Father's eternal promises—forgetting that He is not hiding from me, nor is he withholding the bread of life I so desperately desire. He just wants to be asked.

At this point, I began to see the pain on the road of obedience God called me to. Instead of trusting in His provision for my heart, I would make a slight detour and quickly try to survive on my own.

Do I always give Sister everything she asks for? No. Even if she wasn't happy, I wouldn't make her toast. Instead, I pointed her toward the things in her drawer I already provided for her. At that moment, the construction of a new layer of trust began. As her earthly provider, I must remember—even though I want to give her everything she wants—temporary comfort only masks her greater need. Perhaps providing everything all the time creates more hurt. Masking pain and fear with temporary pleasures and "needs" snuffs out the healing process. When God says no, or doesn't provide in how you find comfort from your greatest fears, maybe His greatest desire is to walk with you *through* those fears.

When fear creeps in, don't waste your energy climbing, scheming, and moving things in your life only to receive burned toast. Instead, invite God in. Allow Him to redirect your eyes to the blessings already laid out before you. Remember His promises in Ps. 16:11, "In His presence there is fullness."

Don't hesitate. As you sit with Him, ask, fully believing He wants to give what's best to His beloved.

Chapter Five

It Is Well: Lament

Dear Sister,

The deeper I enter your world, the rawer I see my true self. I see my selfishness and ignorance, but I have a deep desire to take it all away for you. How can I make your soul well and at peace? Can I do enough, be enough, or promise enough to allow you to experience it? The more I witness your pain and your story, the more I feel it. I carry it. When hurtful arrows come flying your way, causing yet another wound, I am now jumping in front of them, acting not in my character. You have opened me up to a new piece of myself—a warrior of sorts—willing to jump in front of anything lodged at you to lessen your pain. Somehow, you still sparkle when you smile and bring laughter into a room. Your strength is a constant reminder of how much I have to learn from you.

I understand my DNA is not changing into something similar to yours, but my heart no longer looks the same without you in it.

I've made us a routine on hard days. You love McDonald's and a good tickle fight. You also love to sing and have fallen in love with the song, "It Is Well with My Soul."[5] You know every word. When I turn it on, you instantly prop your shoulders back, tilt your head up, and start screaming the words, "It is well with my soul!"[6]

Your hands wave in the air, your head rocking back and forth to the beat, with your eyes closed tight. When you sing this song, it's as if your soul is lamenting to the Lord. I hesitate a bit. It's hard for me to sing those words and to make myself mean them. But you baby, you dive right into the deep end, belting out to God!

I will never forget seeing your tiny little body fully engulfed in worship in my back-

seat. I don't know how you knew the words. I don't know if you understood what they were, what they meant, or who you were singing to, but I saw your heart being healed by the only One who could. You were so caught in that moment, a feeling of peace lavished over you, as if you were in your own little world, just you and God. As I watched you, you taught me how to let go and be real—to show up just as I was, even if I fumbled over the words and wasn't sure if God was even listening.

You have experienced the most beautiful presence with the Heavenly Father from the tiniest age. I had never thought of our Father's presence with those who don't even know Him yet, but no amount of knowledge or age separates us from the love and company of the Father. I got to see God comfort you on those hard days, and He did it in a way I never could!

If the rest of the hard things in your life lodge arrows at you trying to inflict yet another wound, just remember this: God sees you and is with you in ways unlike anyone else can ever gift you. Remember the yummy cheeseburgers, the feelings of happiness in a tickle fight, and yes, even a hug from someone you love. These things will only ever be a bandage over *the pain. Only God can comfort you through the sting of those wounds. He will get you singing words you don't yet understand leading your soul to Him! Don't forget that God's gift to us isn't always in taking the pain away, but in being with us in it! He's right there waiting, waiting for you to cry out to Him. In return, you can cry out, "It is well with my soul."*[7]

I waited patiently for the LORD; he turned to me and heard my cry. He lifted me out of the slimy pit, out of the mud and mire; he set my feet on a rock and gave me a firm place to stand.

(Ps. 40:1–2)

When peace like a river, attendeth my way,
When sorrows like sea billows roll
Whatever my lot, thou hast taught me to say
It is well, it is well, with my soul
It is well
With my soul
It is well; it is well with my soul.[8]

I hunched over a mound of paper files I pulled from the furthest part of my closet. Hours earlier, a grocery store clerk asked, "How big was your daughter at birth because she seems so tiny for her age?"

Her question stung. The clerk asked an innocent question, unaware my mama's heart ached to know the exact answer to her question. The most basic things seemed to pinch the hardest, reminding me of our realities.

Facing me in the shopping cart, Sister looked up and asked, "Yeah, why am I so tiny?"

It was time to face the truth I knew the hidden documents contained. I needed to brave the answers to some of her questions.

Between the chaos of all the new things happening the first day Sister joined us, the trash bags needing to be unpacked, and my heart too fragile to dive deeper into history, I left the paperwork unopened. In fact, I hid them in the closet. Knowing what those files contained, reading through them felt like peeking into a stranger's bedroom window. To read them seemed to me just another way to violate Sister's privacy. More so, I feared all the things I imagined thrust Sister into foster care. I possessed little confidence my heart could love and forgive those who made the mistakes and decisions that resulted in Sister's removal. I felt as if knowing the whole truth compromised my place in Sisters' life.

The whole truth—it's painful.

I entered the foster care world knowing I might not be the right person for the job—not because I couldn't provide, but because I couldn't forgive. In my heart, I felt sure some things are just too big for that to be possible. A needy child I can handle, but an abuser, neglecter, addict, criminal, fill-in-the-blank who is just as needy and just as much a part of the file's pages—no way. Inviting the unknowns into my family's life made the hidden, judgmental, and arrogant pieces of my heart cringe.

Now was the time. Sister was no longer a stranger needing privacy. Forgiveness, understanding, and reconciliation must happen regardless of my feelings or knowledge of the past. You see, I believed it easier to forgive the sins forced upon Sister's life if I remained unaware of the gritty details. Giving grace seemed possible when my view of her life remained gray with blurred lines. That was a lie. I fell in love with a child while holding onto hate for her parents—with or without the details.

Staring at the file before me, fear washed over me.

What if I couldn't handle the information in Sister's file?

Could I forgive the unforgivable?

Could I forget while we all stand in the same room?

Could I place Sister in the arms of the offender and still trust the process, let alone breathe?

More than seeking answers for Sister led me to those files. The nagging push from God to step into more would not leave me. How could I fully love while holding tightly onto hate? These questions led to only one answer—a heart change. My heart needed to be transformed to experience the fullness of what God had for me as a foster parent and for her as my child.

With a deep breath, I opened the file.

I found Sister's name plastered all over each page—pages riddled with bits and pieces of her history. Trying to understand the language of a police report or a court document felt foreign, like entering another world—a much darker one.

Five pounds, eight ounces. I imagined so many times what her tiny little body could have looked like. As I read those words, every fiber of my being ached to have held her, to have kissed her narrow forehead.

I once told myself the lie that it wasn't my place to grieve the loss of something that wasn't mine—this child in my arms who needed to be in another's. But in that moment, grief knew no rules. I stared at the words, grieving at all I read— things no child should ever endure.

I grieved over her trauma. I grieved for so many missing years. I broke in sorrow for the vulnerable. And I grieved for brokenness and loss.

I wept.

I screamed.

I tore clothes off the hangers around me and threw them in anger.

This anger pulled me with a power of its own. I didn't recognize myself. I had never been an angry person before, but this anger had power behind it, drawing me into a dark hole. The longer I sat in it, the more I felt myself slip away, deeper into it.

Choosing to be a part of my daughter's pain—because that is what a mother does—changed me.

I questioned God. How could she come back from this? How could He allow this?

God's presence seemed miles away from that closet floor covered with papers from Sister's file. I felt as if I uncovered a hidden secret that God was ashamed to tell me. How could He not be? Where was He?

With every doubtful question I threw at Him, God sounded more and more like a stranger I immaturely believed in.

Anger is grief's ugly side. When grief feels like it's slowly killing you, anger takes its place. The anger provides targets to focus on and gives reasons for things you once couldn't explain.

None of the grief I felt would be resolved, so I chose anger.

My soul was not well! How could it be? The very reason I hid from the truth in Sister's story is now the reality creating distance between my Creator and me.

My open hands toward God were now curled into fists of anger.

There is nothing as lonely and frightening as being led into deep dark waters and then pushed out to sea. Can I make it back? With no place to lie to rest what I had read, I transformed that grief into anger and made God the target.

Gut-punched

The lady's voice on the phone was blunt and to the point. My legs weakened as she spoke.

"The case plan has changed, and we would like to inform you that Sister will leave your home in the next few weeks."

I felt gut-punched. She spoke the words I dreaded and feared. A "case plan" is a type of road map toward reunification. Reunification meant separation from us. The flood of emotions crashed hard against the ache in my heart. It felt like receiving the news of death, but no one died. The joyous sounds of Sister playing in the next room still reach my ears but competed with the echo of the woman's words.

"Sister will begin the process of leaving your home."

The long explanation of why and how came with a lot of "ifs," and "buts." I threw questions at her.

"Do you guys believe this is what's best for her? Will she be safe? This is all so sudden and not what the long-term plan was. Can you PROVE she will be SAFE?!"

"This is what we have to do. I am so sorry. We will update you in the next few days."

Click.

With that, the voice on the other end of the line fell silent, leaving me drowning in my grief.

I hung up, ran to the bedroom, and screamed into a pillow.

A year and a half of me protecting, providing for, and falling in love with my girl, gone in an instant.

I grabbed the other pillows around me and hurled them to the floor, no longer hiding my screams. Not an ounce of energy remained within me to hold back the flood of anger I kept shoved down inside. The advocate mommy inside of me was screaming.

No, this is not what's best for her. We are what's best for her!

Biological child or not, whether for a week or a year, loss is loss. It's not as if sorrow, measured by the time bonded together, somehow equals an expected amount of grief. Loss is loss. Sorrow is sorrow. Grief is grief.

As a foster parent, you ready yourself to hand a child back, broken-hearted but trusting that the family God made first would be mended. Fear of losing your foster child can never hinder reunification—a child going back to their biological family—and that was never our plan for Sister. As we fell in love with her, we deeply wanted what was *best* for *her*, even if that meant her leaving our home and experiencing immense loss. All of this made perfect sense to me—until it didn't. When decisions and steps to mend the brokenness of a family with the goal of restoring the unit are replaced by a few checked boxes and fear, it sets off alarms. We did not base our concerns on any preconceived notions or history, but what was not happening devastated us. Foster care. It's designed to heal, educate, and reunify families from sins of the past. Cory and I were both learning how to build a bridge for Sister to one day do that. The timing made no sense. It was unjust. It was dangerous. It would make our girl vulnerable again.

"God has not been trying an experiment on my faith or love in order to find out their quality. He knew it already. It was I who didn't. In this trial He makes us occupy the dock, the witness box, and the bench all at

*once. He always knew that my temple was a house of
cards. His only way of making me realize the fact was
to knock it down."*
(C. S. Lewis)[9]

My house of cards collapsed and felt like a trial of faith.
Will she survive? Will her faith proceed after this? I didn't
know!

Lament

I tried to focus on everyday activities, doing my best to nav-
igate the rest of the day. I busied myself doing normal things
like making sandwiches, smiling, snuggling, cooking, cleaning, pretending, all the while holding my breath.

Later that afternoon, panic set in. I needed to breathe!

I laced my running shoes, ready to fight for breath. My
pace was slow at first and my feet felt weighed down. The
anger rushing through my veins pushed me forward. The
faster I ran, the angrier I became. A prayer came out of me
that didn't quite sound like the gentle, quiet prayer I typically
prayed before. It was tense, angry, and loud. It was the broken
groaning sounds of a mother losing her child.

"You say you are peace beyond understanding. Where is
that peace?

"You say you are hope for the hurting. Where is the hope?

"You say you are near to the broken. I AM BROKEN!

"Where are you now?"

As I ran faster, my breath was shorter. Every time I stopped to catch my breath, I heaved over, fighting for enough air to fire more questions at God. Time and time again, for miles I heaved over, fighting for air.

As if to call God to the wrestling mat, I wasn't ready to tap yet. I had more!

"I want justice!"

I then felt the Lord's whisper.

Tell me more. Tell me more Cadey, because I am with you in this!

"I want her safe!"

Tell me more.

"How could you let this happen again?"

Tell me more.

I hurt myself running in such pain, but I continued with a limp. It slowed me, and I eventually crumpled to the mud under my feet. I sat on the side of the road in complete brokenness before God—just Him and me. No more words. Not a single fear of others seeing me, or an ounce of pretending left in my soul—just Him holding me.

It was in that very moment He gently took my grief from anger to lament.

I made my way back to my driveway, looking—definitely feeling—like I had just been in the wrestling tournament of my life. Still, nothing had changed.

God hadn't healed me. He didn't perform a miracle. He didn't take away my doubt or pain. He didn't promise me

I would be Sister's mommy forever. He didn't promise me she would be safe and loved forever. He didn't make a single promise! But do you know what He did?

He gave me His presence. His presence alone held me so tight it chipped away at the anger and gave me breath to breathe in grief instead.

> *When I wanted justice, God gave me His presence. His presence came with the freedom to lament my grief to Him. In every detail, He wept with me. I was no longer alone in the deep, dark waters.*

Friends, I wanted justice. I wanted victory for Sister's life. The brokenness nearly killed me under the realization that it wasn't and still isn't my job. It's His alone. My obedient love for her, and calling her my own, is just a bridge between belief and surrender. Surrender is when you can experience any horrific thing this world delivers, and accept that God will give you exactly what you need in it! Surrendering my anger was the bridge from grief to lament, and it was in that full surrender that God's presence transformed me.

To lament to God is a form of prayer. It differs from weeping. It's different from anger, and it's definitely not hiding. Lamenting to God is talking to God about pain. On that run that day, I experienced lamenting for the first time, and its divine purpose in a painful world. Lamenting was designed to create trust and intimacy between us and the Heavenly Father. Laments turn you toward God when loss and pain can push us to run from Him, to hide from Him, or to point and shoot at Him with sharp arrows of anger and doubt.

We see David lament in the Bible throughout the book of Psalms.

> **How long, O Lord? Will you forget me forever? How long will you hide your face from me?**
>
> *(Ps. 13:1)*

God drew me into a new way of experiencing His presence—a new communication with Him. God was not disappointed with my sorrow and anger. He was not whispering to me to just have more faith.

The questions we scream at God out of the pain we experience here on Earth only have the power to separate us from Him if we let them. God is not afraid or disappointed in our human response to agony. What draws us deeper into the shadows of grief, alone and angry, is separation from Him.

Lamenting is God's way of weeping with us, joining us in the deep, dark waters.

When sorrow hits, when that phone call comes, when your child falls into addiction, when your boss calls you into their office, when your spouse gives up, when your singleness fills the room with loneliness, when you are a target of someone else's sin, when your life's dream has an expiration date, when your family fails you, lament it all to Him. These are the billowing seas of sorrow. God's presence through the lamenting of our souls has the power to make our soul well!

Weeks after my first lament with the Lord, our circumstances were still just as real. We were preparing to say good-bye at any moment. One day, I was in the car with Sister—it had been another day full of activities inching our way closer to our last—when she requested a song, "Mommy can you turn on 'It Is Well with My Soul?'"[10]

How she knew this song, I have no clue. But Sister has the beautiful superpower of hearing lyrics once and knowing them forever. As I turned on the song, she twisted her body in her car seat to better see out her window. I hadn't noticed the beautiful clouds billowing above us until Sister pointed and whispered, "There He is!"

> *When peace like a river, attendeth my way,*
> *When sorrows like sea billows roll*
> *Whatever my lot, thou hast taught me to say*
> *It is well, it is well, with my soul*
> *It is well*
> *With my soul*
> *It is well, it is well with my soul*[11]

Maybe it's the circumstance of being desperate for victory, healing, or justice that will finally draw us into a moment of silence to hear the Father say, *"Tell me more."*

It's then our lips begin to move, and the whispers come forth—it *is* well with my soul.[12]

Chapter Six

Mondays: Hope

Dear Sister,

Mondays—the most challenging day of the week. This day, week after week, we step out of the beautiful and comfortable and see the world for what it truly is—a world right now I fear you'll be returned to. I struggle with uncertainty as I prepare my heart to let you go if I must. In the meantime, we must still face Mondays.

Our Mondays reveal what it truly means to save the lost and broken, comfort the weary, and give grace upon grace—a lot of which happens on this day.

Mondays I see the real you—the past colliding with the present, revealing the ugly stuff hidden, and shoved so far down that it doesn't come out in the typical day-to-day. I see where you came from and release you back into that world with a heavy heart.

On Mondays, my heart aches until the very moment I get you back, and we grow together again. Know sweet girl that through this journey, I SEE you—even the ugly and complex— and I CHOOSE you! Your story has deep scars. Some will heal, and some will numb, but scars hold so much purpose. You have taught me that. The Lord has never promised this life on Earth won't cut and tear away at us, but there is a promise of healing. As you face loss every time you meet your scars, may you remember you are not alone. Continue to build bridges toward the hurting and lonely because, as you have been given hope through it all, others are still waiting for it. Be brave in love. Don't expect those hurting to come to you. Go to them. It's here you will experience God's healing hope in your life.

But those who hope in the LORD will renew their strength. They will soar on wings like eagles; they

will run and not grow weary, they will walk and
not be faint.

(Isa. 40:31)

It was Monday. Ugh. My body ached from exhaustion
deep within my soul and bones. The lack of control in the
unknowns had always been a distant understanding of living
on this earth. However, on Mondays, I felt as if an extra dose
of unknowns was injected into my veins, hitting me like a
poison, slowly shutting down one organ at a time.

Mondays should be a fresh start to the week—a new
beginning of sorts. But for Sister, Mondays meant facing
the unknown of her past, present, and future—the trauma
thrown in her face. Visitation with family—a beautifully
needed part of the journey toward reconciliation and reunification—ended often with an emptiness difficult to describe.

Picture it like a teeter-totter. As a child, you run out
onto the playground. The world is your oyster, some would
say. Your innocence is leading the way. Your eyes search for
someone to choose you to play with. You anticipate someone joining you as you sit on one side of the teeter-totter,
welcoming the joy and connection it can bring. When no
one comes, there is no playing. There is no connection. There
is only loneliness and the unmoved, unshakable feeling of
being unchosen. But then, sometimes, when the clouds align,
someone comes and sits opposite of you. Butterflies swirl in
your belly with anticipation of what it could all become. It

could be fun. It could be scary. Someone could get hurt, but it's all worth it, because "what if?"

On this particular Monday, Sister didn't want to play. Tired and cranky from the coming and going, the unknown, the unfamiliar—it all just fogged her ability to anticipate the joy. She no longer ran with the innocence of the unknown in front of her. She dragged, weighed down by the pain of the past.

Sister kicked and screamed as I buckled her into the car seat. I held my breath as I sat on the edge of the seat next to her, eyes closed, resisting the urge to throw myself to the ground, kicking and screaming in my own melt-down moment. The love-hate relationship of Mondays—when the past, the present, and the future all collide—fear quenched hope more often than not. Even fear collided with fear—the fear of the unknown and the fear of being unable to control any of it.

"I can't do this anymore," I whispered, unaware Sister paused her fit just long enough to hear my words.

"I can't!" She whipped back at me, as if I was the one torturing her.

I swiftly pulled her out of the car, sat her on the ground, and plopped myself next to her. Hunched over in the driveway next to the car, we both sat in hopelessness for a moment before I found the right words.

"Baby, I know you are scared. I am scared too, but you can do this because you are not alone."

When she looked up at me, the hurt displayed all over her face and her eyes pleaded to stay home. Every ounce of me wanted to walk her back into the house and never make her do another complex thing as long as we both lived. My heart wrestled with my mind. I knew staying home wasn't the best thing. It would only bring temporary comfort to her.

So, each Monday, I handed her back.

We both knew I could only hold her hand for so long, and then it wasn't my job anymore. My job was to remind her just because she was afraid didn't mean she was alone. Safety takes on a whole new meaning when you experience its swift ability to come and go without control. We have only so much control. No helmet, protocol, document, or security guard was capable of protecting us from Mondays, because Sister no longer needed physical safety. It was her heart that was vulnerable to assault.

What I quickly realized is that we lack control of our own safety, whether it's the safety of our hearts or the security of our lives. How does a mother, sister, friend, and loved one guarantee complete protection from pain? We can't. There is none. We can provide barriers. We can hold hands as we cross the street. We can teach. We can pray. However, when stripped of all that protection, security, and safety as we know it, blocking our hearts and others from the pain of this world is still completely and utterly out of our control.

We walk around this earth in a false sense of security within our bubble wrap, pretending nothing can penetrate us or the ones we love—until it does. Once the bubble wrap comes off, the helmet doesn't fit, or the body armor is too heavy, we gain a true understanding of just how vulnerable we are to pain.

An unexpected accident, a cancer diagnosis, our parents' splitting, a severed relationship, mental illness, or a broken family (like Sister) reveals our vulnerability to pain and suffering. The sinful assault of this world prowls around us. Who can say we will never be the target of it?

Friends, this is scary stuff. This may prompt you to close the book and toss it in the trash because what our ears are itching for is hope—hope that God will bubble wrap us in His mighty power and gift us with rainbows and butterflies. Am I right? But let's be honest. Anyone who lives on this earth very long soon realizes the perfect life is unattainable here but meant for Heaven alone. However, can I tell you something about discovering your own vulnerability?

As you set out on the journey of acknowledging just how vulnerable you and I indeed are to the pains of this world, you will experience genuine hope in the face of Jesus, here and now!

Don't. Lose. Heart.

Monday Visitations

I had no idea what visitation days would look like until they were right in front of me. After years, they morph and change. They have ebbs and flows, teeter from joy to sorrow. No one prepares you for them. I mean, they do. They (the social workers) share horror stories and give you a schedule of visitation, but they withhold the pain and anguish. They provide just the cold, hard, emotionless facts.

If you've never been in the foster care world, I'll paint a quick picture. If you are a child, they give you a certain amount of weekly court-appointed hours to see your biological family. The purpose of these visits is in pursuit of reunifying and keeping the bond between temporarily separated family members. Visits may take place at the local social services building, a fast-food restaurant, the homeless shelter, or even the biological family's house. The arrangements look a little different for each case and within each city.

Allow me to pause and say this: I share these things only to give you a clearer picture for understanding, not with a judgmental heart. My prayer for you, as I share sparing amounts of details, is that you not only see the world happening right outside your front door, but also that your grace may abound!

If you read or hear details of "the system," or a separated family, and it causes you to cast judgment on what you think is right or best, take pause. I urge you to not only continue to read and educate yourself, but to be prayerful about intentionally positioning yourself in the lives of people who look, act, and have stories different from yours. I have learned that judgment cast on someone, or a people group, without a relationship is like a harness around your heart. It blocks the love abilities you'll need as you walk through this life.

As a foster parent, you prepare the child for these visitation days as much as you can. You dress them to impress because what parent doesn't like to see their child looking cute? And as a foster parent, you use this to communicate your care and love for their child. You pack for the child all the things they may desire as a comfort for them. You imagine various scenarios, so you prepare for all of them. You remind them how much they love their family and bridge the gap between fear, anxiety, and love.

You drive. You wait with them. You pray the Lord comforts them, no matter the outcome. The closer you come to giving your child back for the day, you feel a growing twinge in your heart of something so painful you physically respond. You feel as if a giant ball sits in your throat as you hold back all comments and thoughts. A weight so heavy with ignorant opinions, questions, judgments, love, protection, worry, and loss rests on your shoulders, but you don't dare show an ounce of fear or sadness. This moment for the child is, for most, what they've anticipated all week even though they often do not show it. You force competing thoughts out of your head because the child loving their parents has nothing to do with your love or you. You are protective. It hurts to imagine them getting hurt, but you know your body language and words can alter their desire to bond with their family.

As they become reunited, you experience loss. You refuse to get emotional. This is about them, not you. You remain neutral. The wonky part is that you love the child so much you want them to experience this Monday. You want them to be reunited with their biological family because it is what's best—it's God's first plan—but deep down, the fear keeps you sober about the what ifs and past sins. You kill yourself day in and day out, advocating for their healing and future, even if you are the only one. You feel you would almost die at even the thought of them no longer being in your arms. You weep at the loss of a child because they have become a part of you over the years. The loss feels like an amputation within the heart.

This describes what it feels like to be in obedience to something that seems impossible. Whether it be foster parenting, co-parenting, relational anguish, forgiveness, or whatever.

This is the hard work of building a bridge toward people who may not feel safe, who may not give you control but require an unharnessed heart. This is where I had to learn how to work intentionally to build a bridge of mercy and grace, not a wall of shame and disgrace toward others.

Let me be clear if I haven't been. I do not believe there is a perfect way to do this. I don't believe reunification will piece back together with simple solutions in a lined order. Brokenness is complicated, and loss from each person's perspective within the story is traumatic. Period. This is why I believe

God called our family to foster care. The darkness in that part of the world is utterly hopeless without Jesus in the center. Your intuitions to protect and fight naturally bubble to the surface. Still, it's only when we face them head-on as initiators of the grace we have received from Christ that we can even put ourselves out there Monday after Monday. Bridge-building between brokenness and reconciliation is the believer's job—the church's job—because that's what we have received from Christ Himself.

So there we sat, on the curb, struggling to face another visitation.

Sister didn't know this particular Monday was different. She was kicking and screaming, unaware of a celebration planned there just for her.

Days before, I awoke in the middle of the night in a panic. It was Sister's birthday, and for the first time, the agony of what it must feel like for her family to not celebrate with her hit me hard. Tears streamed down my face as I wrestled with God and grace while reeling with fear and protection.

God, what if I reach out to the family, and it's met with hatred?

Silence

God, it would be so awkward and hard.

Silence

What if, in my selfishness and my pain, I mess it all up?

Silence

God, I will have to do it all alone!

But what if you did?

My step on the bridge I built toward reconciliation, reunification, and love was a birthday party held for Sister, with her family and me coming together to celebrate her.

Once we moved past the sulking and curb sitting, we made our way to our normal Monday destination, but this time was different.

My hands were complete with balloons, a birthday cake, and Sister's bags. Sister walked tightly next to me as we entered the visitation center.

The front desk lady noticed my hands were full, recognized my face, and quickly pointed me in the right direction.

"Mom reserved a room for you guys."

I admit. I was quite shocked because I had convinced myself of worst-case lies. I squeezed the tiny hand Sister slipped into mine as she followed.

We walked through the dark hallway into a cozy room with two chairs and a coffee table full of presents. Each chair was taken, so I placed the cake on the table and the bag on the floor. My tight grip on Sister's hand relaxed as I saw all the smiling faces. I reached for her and placed her on her mom's lap.

I stood in the corner of the room, taking pictures when asked. Occasionally, Sister sent me a side-eyed look and a smirk, as if to say, "This is all for me!"

I returned her smirks with a wink as if to say, "Yes baby—you, me, them, and all of this *is* for you."

Real deconstruction happened within me that day.

What I thought was too scary, too hard, and too painful indeed was. The story didn't end there. We faced more years of pain, disappointment, and difficult journeying, but we met it with hope and healing. So, when we faced more Mondays with kicking and screaming, we faced them with new words and new hope—a new love was there waiting for Sister and me.

> As a prisoner for the Lord, then, I urge you to live a life worthy of the calling you have received. Be completely humble and gentle; be patient, bearing with one another in love. Make every effort to keep the unity of the Spirit through the bond of peace. There is one body and one Spirit, just as you were called to one hope when you were called; one Lord, one faith, one baptism; one God and Father of all, who is over all and through all and in all. But to each one of us grace has been given as Christ apportioned it.
>
> *(Eph. 4:1–7)*

So, we walk about building bridges, not judgment. We talk about loving, not hating. But once the bridge is built, at what point do we stop waiting for the *other* person to walk across?

Many things keep us from getting to the other side and loving with our hands and not just our words. Fear. Control. Anger. Unforgiveness. Betrayal. Ignorance.

What I learned on that Monday—different from every other Monday—is that we will face pain, loss, and disappointment, but to excuse ourselves from becoming the target of it because we desire a bubble-wrapped life isn't protecting ourselves at all.

As I shared with Sister that day, telling those in the world they aren't alone isn't valid unless we are willing to cross the bridge first—or sit on the teeter-totter of life with the antici-pation of joy and connection.

Within each of us lurks the ability to forget the character of God as we witness first-hand the raw, honest display of loss and pain placed in front of us. Imagine what God would do through you if you said yes to the friend who betrayed you, the partner who hurt you, the step-parent who intimidates you, the money you could give, or something else.

The frightening part of saying yes to God in obedience means He not only has one life in mind for you to change, but many. Sister helped me build that bridge toward others with waters of judgment, hurt, fear, and pain all running beneath it. As I crossed, I realized hope is in the freedom found on the other side.

It is here the true healer and protector gains His place in our lives. Once we are no longer chained to our need for control and safety, He can heal with His bravery, His love, His guidance, and His protection. What we once thought would bring us destruction, He used to build a foundation.

Chapter Seven

Judgment: Look up

Dear Sister,

You have a beautiful way of seeing people. I believe it's because you have seen so much. Not long ago, we sat together on my bed. As we so often do during these moments, I toss a question your way, and you give me silly answers. With every ten questions, you'll throw down the most impressive one-liner. Sometimes your answers spark laughter. Sometimes they touch my heart and cause my eyes to fill with tears. You have that way. You are an old soul with a fiery spirit! Once I asked, "What do you think about that person?" Thinking you would throw in a quick-witted joke, but in all seriousness, you looked at me and said, "They struggle to obey, but no one's perfect!"

This piece of your heart outweighs any of your beauty on the outside. May you always draw people in by telling them in your fierce way, "I see you."

Build bridges of love with people who differ from you, and when you feel judgments arise in your heart, lean in and gain a clearer vision of who they are. Never allow your eyes to sink to the floor out of fear or shame. Look up and see the people God has placed around you! They are there for you as much as you are there for them. May you know the Cross has redeemed judgments on your own mistakes. Someone forever welcomed you into a relationship with Him because He built a bridge to you through Christ!

You, therefore, have no excuse, you who pass judgment on someone else, for at whatever point you judge another, you are condemning yourself, because you who pass judgment do the same things. Now we know that God's judgment against those who do such things is based on truth. So when you, a mere human being, pass judgment on them and

yet do the same things, do you think you will escape God's judgment? Or do you show contempt for the riches of his kindness, forbearance and patience, not realizing that God's kindness is intended to lead you to repentance?

(Rom. 2:1–4)

The grocery store seemed to always be a place where people asked ignorant questions and launched painful judgments. With each passerby pushing their cart, I would hold my breath and dodge eye contact. Curiosity often got the best of the strangers around us. It was my job to not only protect Sister from her own impulsive curiosity, but also from others.

After a few trips, I learned to tote Sister in a backpack carrier for the best success—better than seating her in front of me in the cart. In the backpack carrier, she was close, buckled in, and safe. There was no wiggle room for her to lean over and snag things off the shelf, or hop out of the cart once I turned my back. The backpack carrier was meant for a baby, but with Sister's lightweight and small frame, she fit into it just right. With her snuggled up close to me, she was safe, with no attempts at running away or getting hurt. Now, there was a bit of hair pulling on my end, but nothing I couldn't handle.

Often, Sister rested her chin on my shoulder, arms tight around my waist and legs swinging wildly around me. To her, it seemed like a forced place of connection. For me, I took advantage of every close moment, knowing it could be our last. I whispered to her as we weaved our way through the aisles, just for her to mimic me and whisper back. She often cupped her hand around my ear and mumbled nonsense that ended with giggles.

Her giggles and silliness distracted from the looks, stares, and the brave ones who sometimes stopped me.

"Is she your daughter?"

Sister sported a wild head of curly hair. Being bi-racial, she needed specific hair products. So, whenever I made my way down the aisle and began checking out the hair oils, that became their cue to ask whatever seemed to be on their mind about Sister.

On one such trip, I spotted a woman making a beeline toward me.

Here it comes, I thought.

"Is she in foster care?"

I hesitated.

"Yes."

Does the bold woman not see her right here, on my back, listening?

"She is too cute to be in foster care. How did you get that one?"

Really? Why did I even engage in this conversation?

Angry now, I skipped picking out anything for Sister's hair and moved on.

Sometime later, as I stood in line to pay, that same woman—rather persistent—rolled up right behind me.

"So, can I ask you a rather blunt question?"

My mind screamed, NO!

I couldn't object before she launched another painful question.

"Is she a drug baby?"

AARRGH! I whirled around to face her and slapped her across the face!

Okay. Okay. I didn't do that, but oh how I wanted to.

This, my friends, is what judgment can progress into. Judgment has a way of identifying itself as ignorance, claiming that it's okay because once you "get enough information," then you'll decide if you accept and welcome someone different from you—as if needing that information helped place them in the category they belong. Thus, the judgment allows you to sit elevated, untouched, or unchanged, and leaves them in the pit of brokenness. When curiosity is present only to feed one's judgment rather than love, we built walls. Curiosity isn't the thing burning bridges between humans, judgment is. Questions with love can very well be a foundation of commonality between people who don't understand or agree with each other, but it's too often that we allow judgment to lead the way and curiosity curses those around us.

I humbly raise my hand and say I have fallen into this behavior, ignorantly believing I was purely just wanting to know. The reasoning behind curiosity postures our questions as darts thrown or hugs given.

I struggled writing this chapter. I deleted it only to come back and write it again. I keyboarded, holding my breath before finally exhaling with these words because they need to be said.

They *must* be said.

Before we continue, know I am pleading with each of you to start by opening your hearts as learners. Know that judgment, no matter its taken form, can and will block you from the love this world needs. Without looking at judgments straight in the face, calling them out, and placing them at the feet of Jesus, our yeses to Christ produce stunted results, and the grace we give others will be minuscule in power.

I can say firsthand my heart, mind, and worldview of each of these things changed because I choose to live blindly no longer. This is an ugly part of obedience—the transformative battle leaves us feeling beat up and gasping for air. Foster care, although designed as a temporary act of love, should hold a lasting effect on the core of who we are. This truth applies to loving anyone, temporarily or forever. It will change you and the way you see things. You will see things in yourself and others you ignorantly misunderstood before. This is precisely what God designed obedience to look like.

> ### The hard work is just as much within your soul as it is in your hands.

When worlds collide, a messy reality is birthed.

I do not promise to have an ounce of solutions for an entire system and generations of brokenness. Instead, I prefer to share how saying yes to being a part of a long-term solution transformed a short-term mindset in myself.

We are a culture built on short-term missions. Too often, we go in, hold the babies, pray over people, preach the Gospel, and get out before we miss our comfy beds too much. My words may sound harsh, but please stay with me. Short-term missions can be transformational. I've done plenty of them myself and love and support their work and purpose. However, the perspective of a short-term heart cannot speak into long-term solutions. Short-term band-aids the needs, adds strength to the systems in place, brings some healing to the brokenness, but doesn't stay long enough to adopt. Adoption says no matter what, no matter how different, you are now mine. Your pains are now my pains. Your affliction is now my affliction. Your addiction, your trauma, is now a part of who I am.

Short term is precisely as it is. It's the length of time that can only take your transformation so far. We, as a culture, have a SHORT attention span, a SHORT fuse, a SHORT amount of patience.

We see evidence of this when a woman at a grocery store asks if the baby in your cart, or the carrier on your back, is a "drug baby." Unfortunately, this is a common question, and even if not asked, it's a widespread assumption. The belief that all foster children are drug babies, all parents who get their children taken are terrible humans, doing drugs blocks the love a parent has for their child, and all foster parents just do it for the money is part of our "short term" mentality as a culture. We want to peek into a world we know nothing about just long enough to cast thoughts and accusations, but leave before it stains our nice clothes.

With walls standing between communities and social distancing ourselves from one another—from the homeless shelter to the gated community—assumptions are all we have. Until we are ready to cross boundaries and look each other in the eyes, no matter what street we each live on, we will continue to judge one another through assumptions and love only in short-term ways.

Learning My Living Room

As Sister jumped out of the car, she planted her feet and stood tall with intent. She squared her shoulders, lifted her chin, and marched forward battle-ready to face another Monday. Little did I know, I too would take on this posture—a posture that showed strength and bravery while my soul melted.

Hand in hand, we entered the local visitation center and BOOM! Every sensory alarm went off, hitting all at once like a crashing wave, rocking me back on my heels. The stench of cigarette smoke, body odor, and ammonia turned my stomach almost as much as the profanity that flew around the room at high speeds and intense volumes. The overpopulated waiting room made it impossible to avoid the cries and telling eyes of children whose faces and actions reflected their fear, sadness, and confusion.

Sister tightened her grip.

My eyes never knew where to land as they scan the room. Nothing felt appropriate. My brave battle-stance reduced to laser beams on the floor in less than five minutes. One. Two. Three. Four. I counted the nasty tiles at my feet, memorizing their broken checkerboard pattern. I stared at bags on the floor, guessing what might be inside each of them. I analyzed shoes, observed who wore what, and speculated about why.

Sister fidgeted next to me, clinging to the backpack we packed earlier with all the things she would carry with her for the day. I opened it, checked to make sure everything she needed was inside. As I zipped the bag shut, I snuck a glance at a little girl crawling on the floor next to my feet. I noticed her hair, lice caked behind her ears. I recoiled, pulled my hands into my jacket pockets, and then winced at my jerk response toward her.

Week after week turned into month after month. I noticed new things—new scuffs on the tile floor, new shoes tapping on the tile next to me, new voices, new cries. Some weeks, I spent more time in that room with my new "friends" than I would even see my chosen friends. The familiarity in that room grew on me, drawing me from anxious to curious. Still, my eyes stayed down.

My behavior reminded me of a child believing if they remained just still enough, no one would see them—as if to say I can't see you, you can't see me.

Why was I so afraid to look around the room, to look these people in the eyes?

What would I see?

What would I believe about them?

I am here for Sister, and that's it. Nothing more. The quicker I can get out of this awful place, the better! My thoughts exposed a hardness in my heart I hadn't yet recognized.

What I didn't know then was that God had more deconstructing in *my* heart to do. The ripple effect of saying yes to God doesn't end with just one life changed. It's a never-ending work.

One particular Monday, the Lord whispered to me, *Look up, Cadey.* I felt as though God supernaturally lifted my weighted chin. I resisted the urge to squeeze my eyes shut as I gazed around the room.

For me, I felt as if I wore a foster parent sign that stated: Hi, I'm here to judge you or take your child. In reality, I didn't want to take anyone's kid. I didn't want to know their story. I didn't want to smell, hear, and assume the realities of their life. I just wanted to disappear in that room until Sister and I could return to our comfy house, shut the door, and pretend life was peachy.

The room resembled an awful game gone wrong with everyone within their own team preparing to destroy each other at any moment. Tensions pulled people apart. Those who should be on the same team fought like enemies, prepared to destroy one another. Others carried a load of shame on their shoulders as they waited or walked about the room. Eyes looked me up and down, repeatedly, as if to get a read on my purpose in the room. I, too, joined the judgment. I filled my head with made-up stories of where people came from, presumed their intentions, and wondered how it would all turn out.

This is your living room, the Lord whispered to my heart.

My living room? This is nothing like my living room. I don't see comfort. I don't see my leather couch with my two snuggly dogs and oversized, decorative pillows! I don't even feel welcome here!

This is where I've planted you.

I've felt homesick before, but this? This was a gut punch. I welcome others to sit with me. I host. I feed. I comfort. I laugh. I am myself, relaxed in my comfortable, safe environment.

How in the world is that possible in a place like this?

Just look up, and you'll see.

I scanned the room. It seemed everyone played a game with their eyes, looking at someone else until they're told not to, only to later return and investigate further. Every line of expression is examined to judge their subject's behavior and subsequent move.

From adults with badges to children and babies, everyone had something to say and a way of saying it. I read children's faces, their eyes. It felt safer. They were all the same. They all said the same thing.

Sad. Broken. Scared. But what I didn't expect to see was excitement and joy.

Judgment oozed from me.

How could joy be in this place? It must be fake. There must be a mistake, or maybe not, but it is a true tragedy sadness more often overshadows joy on visitation days.

I locked eyes with a little boy who looked to be about ten years old. I studied his body language and face until I noticed his foster mom next to him. He sat close to her as he waited. He clutched his things with one hand and placed his other close enough to hers to show his apparent attachment to her.

Some days, I sat in the waiting room of the visitation center for hours. This gave me plenty of time to story-tell in my mind as I watched.

His hands were fidgety. He swung his legs back and forth, over and over, soothing himself as he rocked. He waited and waited. Stone-faced.

The foster mom leaned toward him.

"Honey, I don't think she is coming."

"NO, she is. She told me she would," his voice elevated.

"Ok, we can wait a few more minutes, but we have to leave soon."

"She's coming. She's COMING. SHE IS COMING!" the boy screamed.

The entire room grew silent. All eyes turned in his direction. His desperation for his mom fell heavy over everyone in the room as the heartbreak triggered trauma in each person's own story. A social worker at the front desk made eye contact with the foster mom as if to ask if she needed help. The security guard took a few steps closer, placing his hands on his waist belt.

An hour passed. Then, like so many Mondays before, the time came that we all watched while his foster mom carried him from the building, kicking and screaming, crying for his mom.

She never came.

I hid my face as tears streamed down my cheeks.

My first thoughts were maybe something like yours.

Poor boy, what kind of mom would do that to him?

We may all, me included, believe we know the "problem." We label her as the "worst parent ever," assuming she should feel shame and guilt for what she's done to that child. We blame her, assume everything is her fault, and label her as the problem.

As a biological mom of three, I immediately thought no matter what, I would/could *never* do that to my kids! I love them too much.

We all have that thing—that one trigger inside us—that will cause us to cross over the judgment and shame line, because deep down we all feel entitled to and want JUSTICE, of course.

Here comes the deconstruction of my judgmental heart. The question that haunted my thoughts as I lifted my chin to see a world I didn't understand: What do others' actions have to do with our calling to welcome them, host them, honor their souls, and love them?

Ouch.

What things could God say about my ugliness and all the times I neglected the important things? Instead, He chooses to welcome me in, be a part of my story, and love unconditionally.

With each week that passed, I continued to brave that "living room" by looking up. I felt the Lord whisper that reminder every time I parked, and my hands shook as I helped Sister from the car.

Every week, I watched this same heartbroken ten-year-old boy scream for his mom before being carried out. It was slow torture, and it took everything inside of me to not scream on his behalf, "Let him out of this nightmare!"

Some days, I inched my way toward him on the bench we shared as we waited, slowly slipping closer and closer to him. All I wanted was to stop his pain, hug him, cry with him, and scream at the people making this happen. Eventually, our worlds crossed, and I started thinking about him, praying over his day. Empathy grew, and he became an essential part of my week. I now knew this boy without even knowing his full name. We exchanged smiles. We even locked eyes at one point. Occasionally, when bravery overtook me, I leaned over and whispered, "it's going to be okay."

Then, one Monday at visitation, after months had passed, the door opened. The little boy's face lit up. He squealed, jumped to his feet, and threw his arms around his mom. The moment he had been waiting for finally came. Week after week, he put all his hope into this one moment he longed for so desperately. And now that the moment arrived, it was as if all the other times meant nothing—just gone?

I felt invested. I felt protective. I had questions. I want to shake this woman hard and give her a good lecture over the agony her son endured because of her actions, but then also hug her and thank her for finally coming. She did it! She chose suitable for this moment, and now he is in her arms where he was meant to be.

She walked over carrying a black trash bag of things. She smelled of cigarette smoke and held a clear water bottle that caused me to wonder what was in it.

Oh, I bet that's why you weren't coming to see your son, I thought.

Ugly judgments filled my mind. Why shouldn't they, you might ask?

I watched as the woman embraced her son and unloaded the bag with things she knew he loved. Then, without hesitation and in all vulnerability, on her knees looking him in the eyes, she just kept repeating, "I'm so sorry. I'm so sorry."

My heart sank. Everyone else disappeared from the room, and for the first time, I felt my judgments for what they indeed were—as if to be unzipped with my heart fully exposed, laying out in front of me. I felt dirty.

Who am I to say this lady is too condemned for this moment?

Who am I to know her whys and her pains?

Who am I?

For the very first time in my life (I'm embarrassed to say), I had a love for a woman I once loathed. I didn't know her. I didn't respect her actions or even support them. However, she was now in my "living room," and with my eyes up, I could see the pain in hers. I watched her on her knees, begging her wounded son for forgiveness.

Often, I believe we judge, and we hold on to unforgiveness because we believe to do otherwise says we accept their behavior, calling it ok. However, that is a lie. In reality, sitting on the throne of judgment only draws a line between them and us, claiming ourselves as more significant and stating they are something less.

I saw myself in her. I thought of the times I've dropped to my knees, begging for forgiveness. Are my failings in the eyes of the Lord any different? Vulnerably, I recognized myself in this reflection and saw the pride in my heart, believing I could not fall so far. It's in our vow of saying, "I would never..." that we lose sight of how far our sin and selfishness can take us.

Separating our brokenness from others' brokenness only perpetuates a cycle of judgment. I was dehumanizing the hidden sins for the "greater" ones.

With the right circumstance, timing, trauma, and pain, we are all capable of doing the very thing we vow never to do. But more so, we are all in need of getting on our knees before the Heavenly Father and plead, "I am sorry. I am so sorry."

The question isn't if a person is worthy because we all would fall short if that were it. The question is more so, are they willing? Look up. There may be someone in your "living room" right now who needs to be seen. And more so, you may find yourself in a bit of deconstruction within your own heart along the way.

> Why do you look at the speck of sawdust in your brother's eye and pay no attention to the plank in your own eye?
>
> *(Matt. 7:3)*

Chapter Eight

Siblings: Hurt people, hurt people

Dear Sister,

It took some time for you to understand what it means to be a part of a pack. It's what the system threw you into when they placed you with us, a bunch of kids with a bunch of craziness.

I remember a week before you came to us. I kept looking in the rearview mirror for four heads, but only counting three. My heart ached to have you in our day-to-day, but my mind couldn't comprehend what that would even look like.

Would they accept you? Would you accept them? Would they love you like I knew I could? I feared they wouldn't follow our lead on the path your dad and I prepared for you. Being a part of the Fenn pack meant all of our things are your things. It meant we're all in, with both feet forward, and I knew the support from our pack would be such a gift to you. I just did not know what it would look like to get us all there.

Then today happened. It was quiet in the house. You had been with us for a few weeks. The quiet made no sense—not in a house with four kids. My mom-alarms went off. Something was wrong!

I searched the house inside and out. Eventually, I found all four of you huddled together in the closet. During a game of hide and seek, you became scared, so everyone decided to stick together in the dark and not hide alone. I am not sure how the game even works at that point, but you guys were having the best time together, and that's all that mattered! So, they changed the rules to have you with them. That was an all-or-nothing moment, and without hesitation, the pack unified.

I watched this same thing happen as we added each of our children to our home, and there is no exception for you. The four of you are as thick as thieves, but baby, I know the more you fall in love with us, the more you realize what you have lost. As much as I know about your life before, I will never understand. I just want you to know that our love for you will never replace or erase God's first story for you.

Know that you are loved. Know that as you brave this scary, dark world—just as I found you today—you are not alone. You now have a pack around you!

I lift up my eyes to the mountains—where does my help come from? My help comes from the LORD, the Maker of heaven and earth. He will not let your foot slip—he who watches over you will not slumber; indeed, he who watches over Israel will neither slumber nor sleep. The LORD watches over you—the LORD is your shade at your right hand; the sun will not harm you by day, nor the moon by night. The LORD will keep you from all harm—he will watch over your life; the LORD will watch over your coming and going both now and forevermore.

(Ps. 121:1–8)

As each day passed, the possibility of Sister transitioning out of our home cast a shadow over my thoughts. I worked hard to push those thoughts aside, trust the Lord, and commit certain memories to a special place in my heart to treasure forever—no matter what.

I remembered the day we told the kids we were going to "adopt." God called us to foster care, but we immediately thought that meant adoption because foster care was temporary, and that seemed too scary.

Hmm. Did you catch that? I feel like we do this with God in our obedience all the time.

We think sure God, I'll say yes, but let me just control this one bit of the story and outcome.

Obedience with only one hand open isn't pure obedience at all. That clinched fist, holding desperately tight to your comfortability and outcome, can steer the entire purpose of God calling *you* in a different direction. I was so afraid— afraid of getting hurt, fearful for my kids to get hurt—and it blinded me from the purpose of love. Love beyond human boundaries is scary, unsafe, and bound to cause pain. What I couldn't quite get past was calling my kids into that exact obedience. How could I? If I wasn't brave enough to tread these waters with both hands opened to God's plan, how could they? How does a mom sit before her kids and explain a stranger would move in, we would call her family, but at any moment she may leave?

We sat the kids on the couch, all lined up, biggest to smallest. I handed each of the kids a piece from a puzzle I made, and together with my husband, we explained we would soon add another piece to our family puzzle. I am almost embarrassed by the emotionless experience we made of it. I now see how far my heart needed to come—the journey God needed us all to take. I now see that in my ignorance, I believed adoption was required to make that child a piece of the puzzle when now we know it's just love.

Sister came to us already experiencing many families, with many additional "siblings" in their homes. I am unsure what reality felt like for her when she came to us. We felt like people visiting a new place and stepping into unfamiliar territory. For Sister, though, one day someone told her one thing, and the next something different. One day someone would be there making promises, and then the next, gone. I say this without shame or judgment. This is the tragic story of most foster children, and it's seldom one person's fault.

To Sister, the people she lived with were a means to an end and barriers to getting what she wanted. To her, every move from home to home validated her sense of feeling unwanted—and a sad "norm" felt by most foster children.

Sister's fight-or-flight mentality and response now dug through the toys with my children, caring less about who sat next to her and more about how she could stuff those toys in her backpack and slip out the front door as fast as possible. My protective instinct did not just disappear because Sister now lived with us. I had to retrain my brain and heart to allow my kids to experience hurtful things. Everything inside of me wanted to bubble wrap them, put them in their rooms, and shield them from what felt like a threat. I relate this to taking your child to the park. Another kid shoves your child on purpose down the slide, or throws sand in their eyes and laughs, but now my child is the one hurting others.

Behavior unaccepted in school or on the playground was now welcomed into the safety of our home. An action that once warranted discipline received a different parental response, leaving my children completely confused. While I understood the hurt inside of a child comes out in hurtful ways, how does one explain that to other children previously protected from the cruelty of the world?

I felt like I was asking them to love a bully, accept her like they do each other, and offer her more grace than they'd ever seen themselves—yet another hurdle I was too weary to hobble over.

"How am I supposed to teach my kids empathy and grace?"

I hurled that question at God as I hid for a moment, locked in the bathroom, taking a timeout from the fighting I'd refereed all day. I continued to plead with God.

"This is too hard for a child to understand."

I had two seconds for God to answer before all the little people discovered me—and He wasn't answering near quickly enough.

Impatient, I threw my spiritual hands in the air and made one final declaration.

"Alright, fine, I am going to make something up, and if I get it wrong and my kids are all messed up, I am blaming You."

While my conversation with God turned a little too honest and cheeky, I know He knew my heart.

Hurt People, Hurt People

I busted out of the bathroom as soon as I heard screaming and found one child crying and another playing, acting as if nothing happened. The offender shall remain anonymous, though the identity is an easy guess.

I assessed the situation and called a sibling meeting—something I had never done before, but as I promised God, I was making it all up as I went. With all eight eyes staring back at me, I announced, "Hurt people, hurt people. This will happen throughout your life, and it's up to you how you want to respond. In this house, we respond to everyone who walks through the front door with love, no matter what they've done or how long they are staying."

I am not sure if they understood anything I was saying, but I surely understood them as my own words came out. I could no longer parent the same, discipline the same, look into their eyes the same. It all needed to change for Sister. So "hurt people, hurt people" became our family motto.

When Sister first arrived, our oldest son, Mason, was seven, daughter Marlie was five, and Maxx, (the baby of the family at the time) was three. By this time, we'd been around the sun many times as a family of six and barely remembered life without her. The adjustments for each of them are a part of their own story to tell, but watching my children struggle to figure out how to love in the most challenging moments—and love genuinely for good—was another prick to my heart. The three of them had their sibling language, a way of playing, and what they loved to do. Sister obliterated that with her entry into our family and created a new normal to schedules and activities. That puzzle piece didn't quite fit snug. We had to shift, cut off some edges, and then re-draw the finished picture together.

As time passed, and the kids grew older, their scars deepened. What was once a couch conversation telling them we would add another child to the family was now their lived reality. First, they pushed and shoved their way into new comfortable corners of the house. Then, like a rebuilt car with a few flat tires, they painfully moved forward together.

The death of my peaceful, perfect family came like a gut punch. The moments of bliss with my children seemed to disappear. I longed to snuggle on the couch under heavy blankets and watch a movie. I begged for God to grow their love for each other quickly. With my heart already rung dry, I had not one more ounce to give. Instead, God found me often on the floor in the laundry room, weeping over the unending duties. He saw me locked in the bathroom trying to breathe after yet another Monday of visitation, coping once again with Sister leaving, only to face more fighting as we came back together. More times than I can count, I screamed into the pillows on my bedroom floor. My family felt messy, my heart was breaking, and Sister was in pain. Death hurts. I cried out to God.

God, this is what I didn't want.

God, this isn't working.

God, if she is going to leave us, how will you mend all of this back together?

One night, I found the three older kids in my bed, completely exhausted and full of hard questions. There were tears, questions, and longings.

"Mommy, why does Sister have to act like that, and you always just give her grace?"

"Mommy, she bites, hits, steals, and sneaks. You never let us do that. Why does she keep doing it?"

"Mommy, how come Sister is so sad on Mondays, and why does it make you cry?"

I took a breath before I answered.

"Well, Sister doesn't understand why she is doing certain things, not yet. Remember, hurt people, hurt people, and we can never really understand how our love and acceptance of *all* of her will work to heal her heart. We should never expect perfection from anyone because (pointing to myself) none of us are perfect."

A funny thing happened that night as I lay in bed, agonizing over the day. My prayer for my kids changed from, Lord, protect them from being broken in this process to Lord, transform their hearts to be more like Yours!

My hands were out in obedience to the Lord with Sister, but were they with my biological kids? I needed to remember and believe that the Lord was the one in control. As parents, we walk around with this false sense of comfort, feeling as if we can protect our kids and shield them from being taken or broken from this world. I released my complete control of Sister's life because I had to. We waited every day for her to be taken from us and learned to live with the looming possibility that one day she could be gone.

What I hadn't released was my complete control of my biological kids. Here's a hard truth. As much as I couldn't control Sister's fate in our family of how long or how many days she would spend with us, I also possessed no control over how many days my kids would be given, who would hurt them, or how. However, I was called to love, and in that love, I could teach them what to do with hurt and pain when it comes. Refusing full submission to God because of my need to shield my kids from pain hinders the heart transformation they will need when hurt comes their way.

My oldest son came home from school upset one day. A girl in his class had been bullying him and making fun of him in front of his classmates. Mason is the kindest and most gentle kid. His heart breaks easily for others, and he loves quickly. He has the most challenging time understanding people's actions if they aren't right. Everything is black and white—I think I accidentally handed that down to him. I calmed him that afternoon with a sweet treat and snuggles, but my emotions drained. I knew my heart barely survived the battles at home, and I dreaded the thought of entering a conflict now at school.

Later that night, we attended an open house at the kids' school. Sister wasn't yet in school, but everyone else was excited to show us their hard work and introduce us to their teachers. As we walked down the street toward the elementary school, my husband said, "Mason, why don't you point out that girl who's being mean to you at school."

Now, if you are a parent, you've probably experienced the heat of anger as it rises from your protectiveness the moment another kid bullies yours. You tell yourself to take a breath because they are just a child. You try reminding yourself that your child is NOT an angel, but still you seethe, how dare they?!

"Cory…"

His name dragged a little coming off my lips—my polite way of reminding him that this kid is just that, a kid. What was he expecting from this introduction, or worse, conversation? What was he going to say? Cory, a towering six foot five, is already terrifying, but to a third-grade girl? This would not go well.

While I wrangled Sister from one end of the playground to the other, Mason pointed at a little girl playing alone on the tetherball court. Cory made a beeline toward her, and before I could stop him, stuck his large, bear-like hand out toward her to introduce himself. The girl looked up, neck cranked, and locked eyes with him. She looked down at his hand, confused, as if she'd never shaken hands with anyone. A smirk twisted upon her face that sent an obvious message that a handshake would not happen.

I then noticed something—her aloneness on the court. My eyes jerked to her tattered shoes and weathered backpack. I looked into her eyes from afar. A familiarity was there.

Immediately, I knew. I could see in her face the harshness and the pain.

Cory's words reached my ears.

"Where are your parents?"

Her eyes dropped to the concrete.

"I don't know. My foster parents are coming though."

Silence.

"I don't even like them though, so I'll probably be moving."

My heart sank as we circled this girl. She stood there so confidently, with fake pride, chest puffed up as if it made her taller. I recognized her body language. It was telling. She was a soldier who had been to war many times. Understanding settled on each of us as we stood there. I watched as each one of my kids glued to her gaze. Carnival games, tetherball tournaments, and chaos happened all around us, but at that moment there wasn't another care in the world but for her.

We invited her to come along with us from room to room. She rejected without hesitation (not a surprise). Instead, she disappeared into the growing crowd of parents and families gathered, taking pictures, and moving from one place to another.

I squeezed Sister's hand as she nestled her body a little closer to me. I knew what she was thinking because I was thinking it, too—the agonizing question of whether Sister would leave, too?

My throat swelled shut. A quietness settled among us for the rest of the event.

As we walked home, my son broke the silence with the healing words I had no idea I even needed to hear.

"Mommy. Mommy. MOMMY!"

His emphatic address brought me back from the mental fog I had slipped into, absorbed in my own thoughts.

"Sorry, yes son?"

"I get it now. Hurt people, hurt people. It's not her fault she's mean to me. She doesn't know how to be nice. Maybe it's my job to show her."

A thoughtful smile curled on his lips as he spoke, and my heart beamed.

Within the brokenness, pain, and hurt we all felt that night, God interrupted it with redemption—teaching my son when I was too tired and weak to do it myself.

A lightbulb switched on in my son's head and heart that day and a new lens of viewing others fell over his eyes. I realized the illumination myself as well. If we want to lead our kids into the heart transformation we desperately want for them, we must do it first.

I moved my family out from behind the barrier of protection I pretended we had.

I had believed the lie that peace within my family was only possible outside of hurt and discomfort. I felt protecting my kids from the world would prepare them to live in it unscathed and without scars. I now know there is no saving the people you love from the hurt in this world. That will never be a job given to the human soul because it has always been the job of our Heavenly Father. I know now that the better work, transformational parenting, and love come from preparing their hearts for hurt because a certain peace comes from watching your child love out of bravery and not fear. There is no scar too deep, no pain too big to be discipled in love—nothing can overtake it.

If we try to take the place of the Lord's care, we will only hand down, through generations of descendants, a false sense of protection from the scary and painful things we face in this world. We can only defend and protect our families for so long before this world penetrates its safety nets. Whether someone or situations through foster care, sickness or disease, your job, your neighbor, or someone in your family, causes disruption or division, we must know our safety is not found in some comfortable peace we create for ourselves. Ignoring the bully, or pretending they will never bite, only sets us up to respond outside of what God calls us to: LOVE.

Chapter Nine

War: Grace Upon Grace

Dear Sister,

You sat with me on the bed today after finding scissors at the church childcare and decided it would be an excellent idea to cut all your shoelaces. I'm thankful someone saw you before you cut everyone else's. When I came to pick you up, you looked at me wide-eyed because they caught you red-handed in your naughtiness (though I wanted to laugh). I asked you, "What do you think I should do, babe?"

It was a rhetorical question, but you quickly replied, "Give me grace!"

I couldn't keep from scooping you up, giggling as I hugged you, because you were so darn serious and proper! So often, the correct answer is grace, and I hope you grab that as truth over your life forever. You have quickly picked up on the family mantra: Grace upon grace. My prayer for you is that you hold that in only to give it out to everyone around you!

You live life on the wild side, pushing every boundary and lifting every rock to see what's under it. It's what I love so much about you. In that wild, adventurous heart of yours, I hope you will learn the need for grace, and for it to take its journey from your head to your heart.

As I'm sure you'll go to the ends of the earth just to see and experience what the world offers, my desire for you is that you learn to look into the eyes of people and see them with lenses of grace—as your story and my love story to you so intricately taught me that.

Grace is what you will chase your entire life, always hoping others around you will choose it as you tornado your way through. Grace will be what you will need as you take a long look into your history and who you are. Grace will be what you will live through to forgive and be forgiven. Look to your Heavenly Father as the ultimate giver of eternal grace just for you and as you draw nearer to Him. The darkness of this world, the things you will never under-stand, won't feel so scary wrapped around the gift of grace!

You, my brothers and sisters, were called to be free. But do not use your freedom to indulge the flesh; rather, serve one another humbly in love. For the entire law is fulfilled in keeping one command: "Love your neighbor as yourself." If you bite and devour each other, watch out, or you will be destroyed by each other.

(Gal. 5:13–15)

Sympathy, Empathy, And Grace

Experiencing the ugliness of having a judgmental heart can leave us haunted about ourselves, chained by our thoughts, and trapped in our own heads. What is our way out? How do we move past a trained thought-life riddled with judgments, caus-ing decay within our hearts, and quenching our abilities to love? Some of us, including myself, cannot see how trapped we are in this. Only by God's grace, as He gives us a front-row seat, do we see how destructive it is to our souls and those around us.

What's next?

Judgments lead to shame, and shame prevents empathy. Without empathy, we cannot move our hearts to a place of grace. Grace leads to freedom, and freedom allows us to love without the suffocating walls of judgment surrounding us, chaining us in our thoughts. We can't just jump from judgment to love without empathy and grace involved. Without this process, it's only words.

We can easily believe the lie that sympathy can replace empathy. Because we can hand sympathy to a stranger on the corner, it gives us a little pat on the back as if we did our Christian duty to love.

However, no one wants sympathy. Everyone longs for empathy. Sympathy walks up to someone stuck in a deep dark hole, feels sorry for them, leans down, and yells, "I'll be praying for you," and then continues walking.

Empathy sees someone stuck in a deep dark hole, grabs a ladder, climbs down, and sits with them. Empathy joins in close enough to see all of them and says, "I love you. I am here with you." It's when we sit close with someone in their darkest moments that we see the birth of grace.

Grace does not erase all the consequences produced from the offender's actions. Grace replaces our need to see those consequences played out as an act of justice. Instead, grace pushes and pulls between the offended and the offender, wrapping them both in love. To be so intentional in loving others—including strangers and those alone in a dark hole—it's a given that their choices and behavior will offend us more than once.

Praying for a heart of grace and mercy is a great start, but allowing the Lord to refine the sharp edges of who we are is the painful, yet intentional, process God designed for us. This means climbing down into the dark holes with people and drawing close to them in their darkness. God provides us with what seems like impossible love relationships, knowing it's not only going to change them, but change us as well through the process. Beauty from ashes will be the outcome with Him. No heart is too broken, no relationship too damaged, and no number of mistakes or severity of sin too much for God to run out of grace. The question is, how do we take the grace given to us and lavish it on others?

God designed us to experience transformation toward love—not stagnant, not unchanging, not set in our ways claiming, "This is just who I am." Do not believe the lie that says internal love is the most important. This type of love may cause our minds and hearts to scream that some person, situation, or circumstance is unjust or not safe. You may hear, "But have you not seen what they have done?" or "Do you not know who they are?"

Once we arrive at the love God intends for all of us to give, the only unfair part will be that we didn't experience freedom at its fullest in our past. We will realize how much time we wasted giving empty love rather than the kind of love given by Christ's example on this earth, and His willful sacrifice on the Cross.

Grace is the first step toward love because it was by grace alone that we could experience God's love as His beloved.

Little did I know that saying yes to being a foster parent would mean getting my doctorate in grace school. I was failing at many of the assignments. I needed intentionally to show up, learn, listen, and sit in the presence of the Lord long enough to receive that same grace for myself.

My Assignment

As quickly as my eyes closed, they opened. The doom of seeing a pitch-black room meant I still had hours before the sun would rise. Sleep was the only place my mind would rest, but there was never enough of it. I lay alone in that dark room, given over to my greatest fear.

Would my daughter be leaving today?

My mind raced and my heart ached from the constant chaotic pace it now lived in. There were never tears—those ended months ago. It was panic that now took its place. My jaw, sore from clenching my teeth, proved even in my sleep I was mourning. My entire body reflected the agony of the unknown fact, but quite real possibility of losing Sister.

My first panic attack left me on the floor, begging my husband to call 911. I thought I was dying. The trauma from the years of this journey wore hard on me. Panic crippled me daily. I knew it wouldn't lead to my death, but panic and anxiety are like driving to death's door and being left there to decide how much more you can take. It's crippling.

It was here God stepped in. On this day, my panic-stricken, tired, and weary body held a soul that had nothing else to give—yet He did.

The walk into the family services court waiting room always felt dark, not like the lights were dim though they were, but more like stepping into the pits of hell. This time was no different. Someone brushed against my arm and squeezed past me. The fighting, weeping, screaming, and cheering—which felt so out of place and awkward—created vibrations in my chest, already threatening to squeeze the breath from me. I searched for seats, avoiding the anguish-twisted faces of women just minutes after being told they were no longer mothers. I scanned the room, never lingering on the children sitting in their nicest clothes, looking around the room with trauma-filled eyes—or downcast staring at tiles—anxiously awaiting their fate from yet another someone in their story.

Tension grew as all the trauma from separation and frustrations fed the anger building in the room. Voices traveled and stories reached my ears.

No escape.

I felt as if I was suffocating.

I clenched my sore jaw tight.

I caught myself holding in all the air—stale with body odor, lingering cigarette smoke, too much cologne, and every aroma from every walk of life—until my lungs burned and the sting forced me to release it. Upright, shoulders tight, fists clenched, I breathed in, slow, and held another.

Finally, we found seats and settled in to wait for our turn on the docket.

My mind raced as I scanned the room, noting every type of person, race, religion, and lifestyle. People talked any way they desired, and at volumes, they pleased. Some entered with police officers by their side. Some came in from the streets. Some wore their best attire, some didn't.

"Love your neighbor as yourself," Galatians 5:14 proclaims. These people, all of them, were my neighbors—the ones sitting closer to me than a neighbor, the ones shouting, the ones being escorted, the ones I knew nothing about other than what I observed at that moment. During my first visits to family court, I wondered how love grew in a heart when all I saw was war and darkness.

I once held up my judgments as proof for justice in Sister's life. It felt wrong, all so wrong. Don't judge. It's such an effortless statement, but it challenged me. How do I love, and not cast judgment, with war raging all around? Judgment held a tight grip on me because I wanted to go to war for my girl and fight with all my might. Only God could loosen the hold this had over me because I was afraid—too afraid to change my heart. So, He placed me on a track toward the deconstruction of my heart and began teaching me how to love through grace despite all the wrongs right in front of me.

Court wasn't new to us. We had been many times. There's never a way to prepare for what comes. This time, as we sat there, I realized those who were once strangers were distantly familiar. I recognized faces from the local homeless shelter Sister visited often. Parents I had once seen in conflict were sitting side by side, squeezing each other's hands. I noted other familiar faces from Mondays at the visitation center. When I caught a few eyes staring back at me, I dropped my head and counted the tiles on the floor at my feet.

"No, NO, NOOO!"

The women's screams brought my mundane counting to an abrupt halt. I snapped my head—along with every other head in the room—toward the woman as she fled with her son in tow, then intercepted and detained at the security checkpoint. Her wailing continued louder while the rest of the room hushed for the first time since our arrival. Time seemed to stand still. All eyes watched as this woman screamed, cried, and wailed in despair over her child.

I recognized that panic.

I was *in* that panic.

My own thoughts puzzled me. Years ago, I would have labeled the woman trying to escape this hellhole with her son as an awful Mom/person, unlawful, and completely neurotic. However, in my perspective and experience as a foster mom, I thought I've wanted to do that once or twice. Maybe that's what we all want, just to grab our loved ones and run!

Perhaps the birth of empathy came from sitting in this family courtroom so many times. Is it possible that seeing familiar faces, hearing their stories, and watching firsthand how unfair the system could be—or seem—bound my judgment and released a new life of empathy within me? Oh, how unimaginable and unbearable it would be to be separated from your child. I no longer saw that woman as a stranger. Instead, I saw a bit of myself in her. My judgment faded and my heart ached for her and her longing to be with her son. The only cause for her to act in fight-or-flight mode is because of the war raging around her—from her perspective, no one seems to fight *for* them.

We all sat in that courtroom waiting area with one common thread among us—each fighting for what we believed was right. Being a foster parent with no rights, my fight took place in my mind and heart. Whether for or against, whether to the end or temporarily, whether for justice or with lies, every person standing or sitting in that heated waiting area had someone or something they were fighting for, and to tell their truth.

My thoughts kept coming at me.

Everyone in this building is at war; is that what God had for me too?

Did all of this obedience and my love for Sister come down to this?

It doesn't have to be this way, right?

On this day in the courtroom, my job as an advocate would take all the bravery within me to be a truth-teller. I had to choose to let grace change the love I had from the inside out, leave everything else at the security check-in, and come in with the reality of what I had seen and experienced for years of Sister's life.

Now, what they didn't know is that "truth" for me was being transformed, as God allowed my heart to be broken for things I believed were unforgivable. My heart ached because I saw the whole story, the entire system, some of the darkest parts of our world, and the judgments placed on people—like us, you and me. I did not understand how one extended empathy and forgiveness to those accused of the worst of sins. What once brought me immense anger and vengeance for justice for the innocence of Sister's life now just feels like brokenness. My heart broke for the consequences of the sin in that room. That moment became my first step toward understanding true grace. Rather than experiencing a sense of "I feel sorry for you," it's more like "my heart is completely broken in the most confusing, yet authentic way."

Relying on what God allowed me to see in this complex process of foster care finally allowed me a voice to speak out. For the first time in my life, I swore an oath with my right hand held high, before a room full of men and women who also all had an opinion on Sister's life and future. Whether a first- or second-hand account, each person had been a part of Sister's story, some longer than me, and some not a part of her life, but all of it. For me, the most important people in that room were the ones who tried to love Sister the best they knew how—family, caretakers, lawyers. Every judgment in that room had a voice at the table regarding Sisters' future. Each held the nasty sin of another to prove a point and win a fight. For me, telling the truth in love and grace was a war fought against darkness, not a single person.

The judge sat to my left. I locked eyes with my husband, who sat in the gallery directly in front of me. I shivered, unsure if it was from the chill in the courtroom, or because the air felt thin, and my lungs felt empty. The tapping of the Stenograph bounced around the room as the court reporter keyed every word. Stiff, and business-like, decisions were made about Sister's life as if it were a business transaction—such a contrast to sitting in a living room having a family meeting.

They gave every person in that room their turn to tell their truth. In God's refinement of my heart during the last years of this process, I understood I wasn't there to prove anyone wrong. I wasn't there to tell a story or even fight for what I believed was suitable for Sister. My instinct as her foster mom was to fight. But through braving the tracks of love God set me on, I knew only grace would set us all free from this messy, painful process. Only the Heavenly Father knows what's right for Sister's life. Only God sees an eternal perspective and holds the truth! My job wasn't to go to war but to love through grace.

When the lawyer lodged his first question at me, my throat immediately closed. I closed my eyes and heard the whisper of the Lord.

Grace upon grace, Cadey.

I answered. I pinched between my thumb and index finger for each question, trying to hold back the tears. I responded to questions regarding the years of history with Sister and all I had witnessed. I held each word with the weight it deserved. A woman will lose her child today and no one deserves that kind of pain. These words matter. First, I ached for the mother sitting in front of me, and I ached for my own heart.

Not like this. It doesn't have to be this way! I tried hard to turn off the thoughts, but they kept coming.

I felt the manipulation of the questions thrown at me, trying to get me to pick up my sword and fight. I wanted to defend myself. I tried to protect others. I wanted to tell the story of why or what happened. I wanted to spew darts at the ones treating the process as an inconvenience or job. I wanted to scream on behalf of Sister's innocence stolen and the trauma she endured. I wanted to jump on the table and act like an absolute lunatic, just to get everyone to snap out of the robotic haze they were in. Instead, as I answered each pointed question, my words cut through the courtroom. It took everything in me not to scream.

STOP!

Stop twisting words!

Stop with the agendas!

Stop pushing shame and blame around this room!

Just stop!

The words were loud, but only in my head.

I wanted justice, yet I also wanted peace. War was not the answer.

The questions finally ended, and a court official escorted me to the gallery. As I took a seat, I felt peace fall all over me.

Maybe it was impossible to stop the war happening in that room, and in the system, but through God's grace, He made it possible to bring peace from grace and love within my soul. Freedom came for the first time, rushing over me like a wave.

Friends, this world will never stop being at war with one another. The only thing the world knows how to do is point the finger. The only policy this world can come up with is to fend for yourself and the few you love. Lawmakers and judges are not paid to give grace a try. The broken system will stay broken because we live in a broken world. It isn't up to this world to free us all from experiencing the pits of hell here on this earth. It's up to us, the ones who have experienced being God's beloved!

That day in the courtroom, judgment and shame pushed from lap to lap. It felt hot as hell—like the hell it was that day. On that day, I decided I didn't have to be imprisoned in it any longer. Grace set me free.

Are you tired from the judgment, the shame-game, protecting yourself from hell here on this earth? It's exhausting. It's lonely. It's miserable. There are a lot of things that will keep this world continually spinning in this war of hatred.

> *What if each of us took grace, not only from Christ for ourselves but also for others—purposing the grace we have received and holding it out to others without condition?*

One person may not possess the power to change an entire courtroom. One person may only have the ability to change one life—their own. You must start with yourself. Receive eternal grace and claim forgiveness as yours and be washed clean. Only then can you be free enough to give that same grace and love to others—those around you who are your neighbors.

Sometimes, when we step off of the tracks God set our hearts on, we lose ourselves. Our instincts and pains may block us from living in the eternal perspective that God is our defender, provider, and Heavenly Father. As much as we want to control what we believe is best and right, when we take that control ourselves, we lose the ability to live in grace and love. Judgment, shame, and pride lead our hearts down a destructive path. Only when we surrender to our Heavenly Father are we led to freedom.

Maybe, like me before Sister entered our world, you've never experienced the need for this type of grace because you've never changed your view of the world. Maybe the five-mile radius from house to work, and the people you rub shoulders with, never change. Mine sure did, and what I saw in myself wasn't Christian. It was worse than that, and it wasn't holy. It was dark.

The God who placed grace upon grace over our lives doesn't give our imperfect selves the freedom to determine who receives that grace. Instead, He gives us the freedom to decide who will be our neighbor. We can live with our eyes down, shielding ourselves from ever looking into the eyes of the faces around us. We live in a world where we build block walls from house to house. We pull our cars straight into the garage and lower the door before the light from the outside can seep in. We live behind locked gates, double pained windows, masks, and face shields—only to interact with others if we choose. God will never force you to set your heart on the tracks of grace toward unconditional love. We must choose it. We must look up, be intentional, move into the neighborhoods, spaces, and relationships, knowing we aren't there temporarily. We must move from the shallows into the deep. Grace doesn't need to be given in shallow relationships. We need grace when we are barely keeping our heads above water. That's when grace is our lifeline.

Chapter Ten

The Backpack and The Wedding

Dear Sister,

You have been through hell and back. You have seen the unspeakable, endured a broken spirit, and experienced continual loss. You have been moved to countless homes, slept in many cribs with many unfamiliar arms holding you. You sit on laps and walk around rooms as strangers decide your future. We have been a part of that. You came to us as a stranger, a visitor to our home. We hoped God would give you a forever, and that we would get to be a part of whatever that looked like for you.

I see the longing in your eyes to just be like everyone else, to fit in, to have a polished story. You try to hide your story and mask it with something new. You point at the pictures on the wall and smile as you remind me your face is there, as if to tell yourself, "See, I belong."

You silence everyone in a room, even if it takes you getting on top of the table and singing, because if we aren't all watching, you feel lost and forgotten. You draw attention to yourself, whether bad or good. To you, it doesn't matter because there is a lie embedded into your mind and soul that says if you don't fight for what you want, you'll never get it.

The truth is, that lie is less of a lie for you because that's how you've survived. You display a longing to be seen by others, but you run because being caught is too vulnerable once seen. Needing and loving others means pain. It means loss. It's what you've experienced.

For two and half years, I have worked tirelessly to prove you wrong in this—to prove to you there is redemption, healing, joy, and there can be singing! My love, no one on this earth can promise you a forever because this life is fleeting, but I can promise you I will always love you. A home or a title does not box in love. Love has no bounds. I will snuggle you even when you look away. I will shine the light on you when you need attention. I will encourage you as you try new things and fail. I will love you even if you don't love me back. I will fight for you even as you come and go from me. I will hold your hand as you learn how to value relationships with others. No matter the circumstance or outcome, my most remarkable yes to our Heavenly Father was receiving the gift of YOU!

Sister, titles will be stripped from you your entire life on Earth, but the one title that holds, no matter what, is your title of beloved. You are the daughter of the highest king, and your eternal inheritance to Him can never be shaken. If you set Him on the throne of your own heart and believe in who He is in your life, He will whisper to you the words that brought me deeper into your story, "I am with you!"

But when the set time had fully come, God sent his Son, born of a woman, born under the law, to redeem those under the law, that we might receive adoption to sonship. Because you are his sons, God sent the Spirit of his Son into our hearts, the Spirit who calls out, "Abba, Father." So you are no longer a slave, but God's child; and since you are his child, God has made you also an heir.

(Gal. 4:4–7)

The Backpack

I found Sister frantically gathering things in her room, zooming from one corner of piled items to the next, with her arms full and a few items clenched between her teeth. Her eyes appeared wild and harried as she buzzed about the room. I crouched down in front of her, causing her to pause and look into my eyes.

"Sis, what are you doing? We have to go."

Today was visitation day, and I did not know how many more would come. I noticed her favorite backpack sitting next to her with all her favorite items spilling from it, including a few of my things. Before Sister opened her mouth to answer my question, I recognized what she was doing. She was packing her bag with love reminders.

As a child without the experience of a forever identity anywhere—never knowing what home would be the next, who was safe or if that person would return—she used this backpack as a place to hold everything she loved and cared about. Within it, she stuffed pictures of people she cared about, a "blankie" she slept with, sometimes a toothbrush, or even a rock she found that meant something to her. The backpack, so full it challenged the stitching, often weighed down her tiny frame as she hoisted it onto her back. She didn't care that it sometimes toppled her over. She just needed it complete.

I once noticed this need of hers to carry my love with her and got an idea. I pulled out my favorite necklace and handed it to her.

"Sister, I want you to take my favorite necklace, not to have it, but to remember that you will come back to me. You can give it back to me then, but while you're away, if you feel alone, you can pull it out and remember that you have a little piece of me with you."

Her shock gave way to an ear-to-ear grin as she stuffed it into a secret pocket.

Each item she placed in that brimming-full backpack held a promise reminding her she was chosen, loved, and cared for. When her mind grew frantic with loss and pain, she would zip it open and see reminders of love—reminders of her identity.

As the months gave way to years, what went into the backpack became too overwhelming. One pack just couldn't hold it all. Each week and each visitation, it became so full and heavy that I had to sit with her and help her decide what was most important. I became frustrated many times with this endless battle-of-the-backpack. My reassuring words to her could not be stuffed into that bag. My tireless service and proven love couldn't be exposed onto the photo of the two of us she carried with her. I worried about her tiny body carrying such weight on her back, and her obsession with needing things to remind her that she is loved.

It was in these things she carried that she felt the most worth. Her need to be chosen, and proof that love wasn't going anywhere, ran so deep that she stumbled around with a backpack far outweighing her little self just to experience a sense of comfort.

What was it about these worthless things that brought her more comfort and reassurance than my promises to her?

We loaded the car. I finally got Sister to agree on the appropriate backpack items, even allowing her to stuff in a few more of the things she found and wanted to bring with her to visitation. The drive took two hours, so we had a solid routine. First, she napped, then a snack and her favorite music to sing along to, and then we made the final thirty minutes of the trip before we had to say goodbye. Each time, I answered a million of her questions and tried my hardest not to cry. This time was different. She didn't want a nap, snacks, or songs. She only wanted to talk. After answering a few questions, I felt my chest tighten and my eyes swell.

"Sis, how about we listen to some music for a while?"

"I have one more question," she said.

"One more is fine."

I waited. She paused for a while as if choosing her words carefully.

"Mommy, can I marry you and Daddy, because married is forever?"

My heart hung a beat. I held my words as I discerned the right thing to say. What I wanted to promise weighed heavily with what her words truly meant, except we hadn't yet been told if adoption was the next step. Promising her a forever with us wasn't a truth I yet held. So, I said what I knew would always be accurate, no matter the circumstances.

"Baby, my love for you will be forever, and there is nothing you or anyone else can do to change that."

I knew it wasn't what she wanted to hear as I studied her in the rearview mirror. Finally, she looked at her backpack, then back at me, and then slowly closed her eyes as if to tell me she was done talking.

The Wedding

Though the conversation was short, the long-awaited call came at last. Visitations were ending, and adoption was now in the future. After all these years, facing the possibility of adoption felt so unreal it shadowed what should have been a celebration. No more back-and-forth trips, no more backpack, no more questioning for Sister. She would finally feel the love and comfort of a promised forever.

Saying goodbye to the world we knew, and the people tethered to Sister's life, came with a gut punch, traumatic for her in every sense of the word. A new normal began, and a broken hallelujah continued. The date for adoption changed multiple times, and by the time the day stuck, nothing felt real.

One night, we stood in front of the mirror together. She insisted on wearing a "wedding dress" the day of her adoption, so together, we spun around in front of the mirror, holding our dresses and dreaming of the day to come.

"Mommy, what will change on my wedding day?"

Would anything change?

"Your name will change, but that's about it."

"Will that make me different? Will I feel different?"

"Well, Sis, I am not sure. But I know one thing, there is nothing you can do for me not to love you."

As we walked the steps of the courthouse, all dressed in our wedding attire, the memories came flooding. The stories told in this building were full of suffering and loss. This most beautiful and awaited day, tethered to brokenness, caused a rush of disappointment. The stories I watched and heard about adoption never showed this—the broken part.

A wave of sadness fell over me as I grasped Sister's hand. My heart held the truth of so much pain leading to this day. The laughing, the smiling, the excitement all came at a cost. As much loss as gain filled Sister's life. My journeyed heart couldn't fight feeling it all, in its heaviest form.

My heart ached.

It didn't have to be this way.

And my heart soared.

She twirled in her dress with no amount of insecurity

holding her back. She shined as the packed-out courthouse cheered her new beginning. She, of course, made the judge gut-laugh with her silliness and brought tears to us all with her honest words spoken. What I saw in my daughter that day was a piece of what I believe Heaven might be like. It was safe, free, and glorious.

I looked around the room and remembered the day I stood up for grace. Slowly, I drew in the musty courtroom air and released a deep, satisfying breath, noting just how far my heart had come. As we signed each document, my mind took me to my closet floor, scattered with court papers, when I read and learned Sister's story.

Only as the judge proclaimed Sister's new name, and announced Cory and me as Sister's given parents, did I return to reality. Glorious as the moment was, I grieved for the loss others had to experience.

Truly, it was a broken hallelujah.

As the sun set on the perfect wedding day—and my daughter was given her forever—we snuggled up together anticipating our newfound ordinary. However, we soon realized tomorrow held the same things as yesterday.

Weeks passed, and a new rhythm to our schedule appeared. I breathed lighter, more manageable, and Sister slept better. Yet every day, I would find Sister in her room, loading her backpack. It was like clockwork, a built-in life support for her, and the promised forever hadn't yet changed her need for physical reminders.

Our culture has believed the fairytales told about adoption—surprised, once again, I had bought into that lie as well. I felt frustrated. Sister wasn't yet free from needing to lug around the weight of her backpack. I soon understood adoption was only the beginning. Each day I watched her as she settled into her routine of frantic behavior, packing her bag full—complete with things that comforted her. I waited with patience until she approached and asked me to zip it closed, then I reminded her we no longer need it.

"You are here forever, baby. We don't need to pack this anymore."

Each day, we decided what items she would take out and never put back in.

Months of this went by until I realized the backpack wasn't doing what it once did for her. Instead, it was a trigger—a reminder of hurt—and seemed to keep us from moving forward. Every day she packed it and picked it up was one more day she didn't bravely move forward to the promises of forever.

I grabbed her backpack one morning before she woke. Today was the day. When she came to me asking for it, I told her we wouldn't be packing it. There were instant tears. I reassured her she could now enjoy those things rather than hide them away and carry them around. We walked together to the kitchen trash can, and as she placed it inside, we whispered, "Adoption means forever, and I am not going anywhere. It's time to unpack."

Could you, beloved, take a moment and hear that same whisper over yourself?

"Adoption to Christ means forever, and God is not going anywhere. It's time to unpack."

Life before the adoption was not erased; it was redeemed. All I wanted for Sister was to enjoy the liberties and blessings of her new adoption. Yet, her new name and promised forever didn't erase her past identity.

We, too, can live that same way—embracing the promised adoption of being Christ's beloved, yet still carrying the weight of what this world told us of our identity:

Broken.

Weak.

Unloved.

Not enough.

Unwanted.

The world leaves us to believe the lie that just being God's beloved isn't enough to live out our purpose on this earth.

I am sure Sister's forever would have come whether or not we became foster parents, but would my forever have changed? The lies I believed about myself kept me from living freely in God's identity of me, which could have kept me from saying yes to God and ultimately saying yes to Sister. Believing the lie could have stolen a love purposed for my life now, and the transformation God chose me for.

What I see now is, without the foundational truth of knowing our adopted identity as God's beloved child, we will always carry the weight of who we aren't.

We will never believe we are the world-changers because God placed us here in it.

The hands of our Heavenly Father held Sister's forever. That was never in my control. What I didn't know was that adoption comes in many forms. Our culture says it's with a judge and signatures, but my heart came to know it as a choice. In that love choice, my yes to her and to what God called me to would never end. My yes to adopting those around me with a love so fierce that it tethers us together requires no signatures. My yes showed me the power of grace and mercy. My yes etched away at selfishness and judgments glued to my heart I never knew existed. My yes transformed my family from only caring about the people within it to pursuing people outside of it. My yes taught me that lament is an intimate gift from God.

My yes took me on the journey more than gaining a daughter. It was gaining the God-life intended for me—wild, free, brave, vulnerable, scared, weak, and human—all while experiencing my true identity in being God's beloved.

What I had hidden in my backpack, because of insecurity in my strength and unwillingness to fail, was unpacked. The freedom that has come from that leads me to believe even if/ when I experience loss, pain, trauma, weakness, and failure, God is with me. Could it be that the end of the story didn't hold as much power as we all thought it would? In the same way, I believed getting to adoption day would finally give me peace and Sister the freedom to live in her true identity.

Dear Sister began as love letters to my daughter, and as they unfolded, I read those letters back to myself. I found the truths in my words to her were truths I also needed to hear. As I started writing this book, I was haunted by how it would end. I knew not everyone gets a happily ever after and a wedding day. For me to challenge the women of this world to say yes to something God is calling them to—something scary that may lead to heartache—kept me up at night.

This book isn't just for the one who thinks they want to adopt. I hope it isn't even for the one inspired to adopt. This book is for the adopted who needs to be reminded of who she really is!

These love letters spoke directly to an orphaned heart, one who desperately needed to know how loved and chosen she was by Jesus. It won't be until your identity as an orphan of this world is held in the arms of Jesus that you will then experience the freedom, bravery, and purpose of saying yes to God, in all things.

God never called me to a purpose, to make a change, or to save a life because He needed more from me. He calls us to say yes to Him, not that we may gain on this earth, but that we gain more of Him.

This book isn't about how much we need to do for God. It's not about accomplishment. It's not even a call to action.

It's about returning you to your first yes to God. Reminding you that His death on the cross and resurrection claims you as His beloved.

Without the foundation of our yeses to God being for His eternal gain, we will continue to live in the "I could never" world. I could never be a foster parent. I could never love that person. I could never forgive what they have done. I could never experience that.

God's desire for our yeses to Him may intentionally lead us to dependence, not self-sufficiency.

Where does yes to God lead us, to more of Him?

I asked myself if adoption wasn't the end of this story, and if it ended with a loss of a child—my child—would it still have power? Would it still matter to be told? If Sister wasn't with me now, would it have all been worth it?

The answer is, yes—a thousand times, yes.

Sisters, yeses to God will lead to pain. They will be hard. They will change you and may even lead you to death's door, but they will always be met with more of Him. That, my friend, is a yes to be told.

Sisters, it's time to unpack your backpack. God is asking you as His beloved to make yourself at home with Him. Replace the identity you have given yourself on this earth with whom He claims you to be.

You will finally get to know who God created you to be when you hold your arms out, hands clenched, and lips saying, "Yes."

Conclusion

It's Now Your Turn

My Letter To You

Dear Sister,

God has gifted you with a messy story that will never be easily mastered, or comfortable. He has also chosen you, knowing all the mess you try to cover up or pretend isn't there. You may carry a backpack full of temporary comforts and love promises, yet it's so weighty you are too weary even to see there is no need for it anymore. You've told yourself that it's the life preserver that keeps you afloat. When you feel insecure or unchosen, you frantically go searching for a reminder that you once were. You've believed the lie that lugging this thing around will bandage the wounds and heal the scars, and that maybe it will make you enough. The truth is, it is hindering you from being free. When God chose you as His beloved forever, He desires to unload the backpack that once made you feel safe, chosen, and loved. He wants for you to no longer live with an orphaned heart but a chosen one.

Beloved, if you saw your position next to the Father as unshakeable, what would your yes to Him look like? If you truly let the words, "There is nothing you can do to change how much I love you," ring true in your ears, what could stop you?

It is in the messiest stories, when unpacked by the Father, that have endless hallelujahs.

Only heroes wear something on their back and hold the weight of saving lives, the freedom of living in our true identity as God's beloved means He isn't calling us to superhero work or looking for the perfect one to use.

You are the one who can change this world—maybe even one person's world—from seeing only brokenness to hope. You are the one who's called, even when your gut is telling you that you'll fail. You are already strong enough because your weakness is God's open door to show His strength. You don't have to live in fear. God is calling you out gently just to take one step at a time. You have already received all the grace it will ever take to give it in return. Your judgment and your past do not have to define you. Allow God to refine it in you. He built you to lament, experience loss, endure pain. Don't run from it, unpack it.

May your wedding day to Christ only be the beginning of your journey. Your identity starts as a named daughter of God. It is there that you hold heir to eternity with Him. As a child, standing on a doorstep with trash bags in hand, we are invited in to be called His, claimed with a purpose, and redeemed from brokenness. It's within the relationship with Him that our wounds, our pain, our trash bags from life will be unpacked and healed.

Sister, may our forever story mean something by our yeses here on this earth!

The Story Continues

Thank you for journeying with me. My prayer is that this is only the beginning for you and me. Who knows where our next yes might lead, or what story will need to be told? All I know is I am ready to meet the ones who have flipped through these pages and are ready to risk it all as they say yes to God. That's you!

I provide FREE devotionals on my website and would love to share with you.

To connect, share your story, or subscribe go to: www. CadeyFenn.com

About the Author

Cadey Fenn loves God, her husband Cory, and her four kids. She serves in women's ministry at her church and is passionate about discipling and teaching women. Cadey works at Onward Leader, a ministry that disciples and trains young ministry leaders across the Country. Cadey speaks from multiple stages, but her number one love is teaching her four children around the kitchen table at home.

Notes

1   Piper, John. 2013. "When the People of God Risk and When They Don't." *Risk is Right*: Review excerpt on back cover, 64. Illinois: Crossway.

2   Wright, N. T., *Paul for Everyone: The Prison Letters: Ephesians, Philippians, Colossians, and Philemon*, [Westminster John Knox Press, 2004] 18

3   Awana (Approved workmen are not ashamed) is a world-wide nonprofit ministry focused on providing Bible-based evangelism and discipleship solutions for ages 2-18. http://awana.org

4   Michael Ford, *Wounded Prophet: A Portrait of Henri J. M. Nouwen*, [New York: Doubleday, a division of Random House, Inc., 2002] 22

5   Sankey, Ira, and Bliss, Philip, "It Is Well with My Soul," *Gospel Hymns No. 2* (1876), Spafford, Horatio, Writer (1873), Philip Bliss, Composer

6   Ibid

7   Ibid

8   Ibid [stanza 1]

9   Lewis, C. S., *A Grief Observed*, [New York: HarperCollins Publishers, 1996] 26

10 Sankey, Ira, and Bliss, Philip, "It Is Well with My Soul,"

11 Ibid [stanza 1]

12 Ibid

A free ebook edition
is available with the
purchase of this book.

To claim your free ebook edition:

1. Visit MorganJamesBOGO.com
2. Sign your name CLEARLY in the space
3. Complete the form and submit a photo of
   the entire copyright page
4. You or your friend can download the ebook
   to your preferred device

A **FREE** ebook edition is available for you
or a friend with the purchase of this print book.

_____

CLEARLY SIGN YOUR NAME ABOVE

Instructions to claim your free ebook edition:
1. Visit MorganJamesBOGO.com
2. Sign your name CLEARLY in the space above
3. Complete the form and submit a photo
   of this entire page
4. You or your friend can download the ebook
   to your preferred device

Print & Digital Together Forever.

Snap a photo

Free ebook

Read anywhere

CPSIA information can be obtained
at www.ICGtesting.com
Printed in the USA
JSHW021725230622
27442JS00004B/6